© Vashelle of Divine Photography

Ruth King, M.A., is president of Bridges, Branches & Braids, an organization devoted to working with negative emotions in positive ways, notably the *Celebration of Rage*™ and *Generational Healing*™ retreats, and the audio CD *Soothing the Inner Flames of Rage—Meditations that Educate the Heart & Transform the Mind*. A respected authority on the topic of rage, she is also a life coach and team-development specialist. Her client list includes Kaiser Permanente, Intel Corporation, and Levi Strauss & Company. King works extensively with managers, counselors, consultants, psychotherapists, educators, trauma workers, practitioners of the healing and expressive arts, spiritual counselors, artists, activists, mothers, and other women and men who influence the lives of others, to transform the emotional body and mind. King works internationally and lives in Berkeley, California. Her Web site is www.HealingRage.com.

HEALING
RAGE

*Women Making
Inner Peace Possible*

RUTH KING, M.A.

GOTHAM BOOKS

GOTHAM BOOKS
Published by Penguin Group (USA) Inc.
375 Hudson Street, New York, New York 10014, U.S.A.

Penguin Group (Canada), 90 Eglinton Avenue East, Suite 700, Toronto, Ontario, Canada M4P 2Y3
(a division of Pearson Penguin Canada Inc.); Penguin Books Ltd, 80 Strand, London WC2R 0RL,
England; Penguin Ireland, 25 St Stephen's Green, Dublin 2, Ireland (a division of Penguin Books Ltd);
Penguin Group (Australia), 250 Camberwell Road, Camberwell, Victoria 3124, Australia (a division
of Pearson Australia Group Pty Ltd); Penguin Books India Pvt Ltd, 11 Community Centre, Panchsheel
Park, New Delhi–110 017, India; Penguin Group (NZ), 67 Apollo Drive, Rosedale, North Shore 0632,
New Zealand (a division of Pearson New Zealand Ltd); Penguin Books (South Africa) (Pty) Ltd, 24
Sturdee Avenue, Rosebank, Johannesburg 2196, South Africa

Penguin Books Ltd, Registered Offices: 80 Strand, London WC2R 0RL, England

Published by Gotham Books, a member of Penguin Group (USA) Inc.

Previously published as a Gotham Books hardcover edition

First trade paperback printing, September 2008

10 9 8 7 6 5 4 3 2 1

Gotham Books and the skyscraper logo are trademarks of Penguin Group (USA) Inc.

Copyright © 2007 by Ruth King

The Library of Congress has catalogued the hardcover edition of this book as follows:
King, Ruth.
Healing rage : women making inner peace possible / Ruth King.
p.   cm.
Originally published: Berkeley, CA : Sacred Spaces Press, c2004.
Includes bibliographical references.
ISBN 978-1-592-40314-1 (hardcover)   978-1-592-40406-3 (paperback)
1. Women—Psychology.   2. Anger.   3. Self-evaluation.   4. Self-management (Psychology).
5. Peace of mind.   I. Title.
HQ1206.K468   2007
155.6'33—dc22   2007014138

Printed in the United States of America
Set in Minion
Designed by Victoria Hartman

While the author has made every effort to provide accurate telephone numbers and Internet addresses
at the time of publication, neither the publisher nor the author assumes any responsibility for errors, or
for changes that occur after publication. Further, the publisher does not have any control over and does
not assume any responsibility for author or third-party Web sites or their content.

To
My family
My world family

～

May every one of us become more curious and less frightened of rage. May manifestations of rage be acknowledged as pain and treated with the greatest compassion possible. May we look at one another's rage, recognize ourselves, and fall in love with what we see. May our good deeds open our hearts in ways that heal the roots of suffering throughout the world for all beings.

CONTENTS

FOREWORD

We live in a world where humanity continues to suffer terribly because we don't know how to deal with anger, hatred, rage, injustice, oppression, and conflict between people and between nations. Yet we also know from the beloved examples of Dr. Martin Luther King, Jr., and Gandhi, Dorothy Day and Sojourner Truth, from Buddha and Jesus, and from our own heart's deepest wisdom, that there is another way.

Ruth King has dedicated much of her life work to understanding the fiery energies of rage, hatred, and fear, and defining ways to respect, understand, and transform these into a positive power in our lives. She has articulated the painful history, patterns, and traps of a raging heart and offers the skillful means for liberation in their very midst. This is revolutionary work.

As a Buddhist meditation teacher, I was first simply trained to mindfully experience and tolerate these energies. But beyond meditation I then struggled with a need to face them head-on, work with them, and express them without creating more suffering. In this book, Ruth teaches and encourages us to be brave, wise, alive, and compassionate, to both honor our rage and its causes and use them to heal ourselves in the world.

May these teachings and practices bring all who read this book relief from suffering and a clear, strong, and wise heart.

Jack Kornfield
Spirit Rock Meditation Center
2004

INTRODUCTION

From Hole to Whole*some*

I've been enraged all my life, but for half of my life I didn't know it. Before I knew I was enraged I considered myself to be a high-functioning professional woman. With a background in clinical psychology and organization development, I worked at some of the most prestigious Fortune 500 companies coaching leaders in how to make effective business decisions and develop high-performing teams. I was educated in some of the most highly regarded institutions of human development. I trained other consultants and was considered a master designer of group development, diversity, and leadership training programs.

While my work was respected, I had a problem with every *authority figure* I worked with. In my opinion, *they* didn't know what they were doing, *they* never gave me enough credit, *they* always fell short of making the mark, and *they* always needed me—whether they knew it or not. Yet you would have been in for the fight of your life had you told me that I was enraged. What I came to realize was that I had unconsciously chosen a high-powered consulting profession to guarantee me the privilege of pointing out to people in authority how wrong they were, and instead of being abused—as I had been as a child—I was well paid, which meant I was *finally right!*

In the prime of my superficial success, I underwent open-heart surgery for a prolapsed mitral valve, a congenital heart condition. I'll never forget how I felt waking up from surgery. I was cold, clammy, and half dressed. An invasive tube ran down my throat and was held in place by tape across my mouth. I felt silenced. There was a blinding light above my head, and needle marks spotted my arms and chest. A large, impersonal machine appeared to be forcing me to breathe. I felt controlled. There were loud sounds from monitors that looked like angry gray monsters. The enormous weight that once lived inside my heart was now on my chest burying me alive. I felt trapped. I panicked and tried to move, but alarm bells alerted the medical personnel and a slew of them filled my room in an instant. Terrified, I thought: *This must be hell!*

Good Morning! Welcome Back! Their eyes and voices were kind as they busied themselves adjusting monitors, bags, needles, and my bedding, and patting the sweat from my brows. *You are doing just fine, Miss King. You are going to be just fine!* I couldn't speak, but my eyes were screaming: *Who the hell are you people? What have you done to me? Get me out of here! I want out, out!* I was frightened, but even more I was angry. You see, I had sworn long before never to let anyone have this much control over me. Yet, these strangers, whom I considered enemies at the time, not only had control over my heart, they had more access to my heart than I did. It was like a nightmare. Dr. Welder, a squat-looking young man, entered:

> We have good news, Miss King. We did not have to replace your heart valve. We were able to repair it. This means there is nothing artificial about your heart—it's all yours! In no time, you'll be as good as new!

But he was wrong! Little did I know, lying in this stark white, ammonia-scented intensive care unit, that this rude awakening marked the beginning of a profound journey from open-heart surgery to an open heart.

During the helplessness and haunting stillness of my recovery, I found myself remembering the war zone of my childhood. I grew up during the height of the Civil Rights Movement in a working-class family with my mother as head of our household. I was the fifth of eight children, the first six of us each one year apart in age. We lived in a thriving neighborhood in South Central Los Angeles. Many families on 43rd Street east of Central owned their homes. Ours, like the others, was a handsome, tidy, single-story, Craftsman-style house with a large front porch.

Success in our community was defined as being obedient, getting a job with the county (instead of being on county assistance), and making it through the day without being harassed by the police. You could not be softhearted. You had to be tough to survive, know how to follow the invisible mind maps of *the enemy*. Having feelings was dangerous, being called a bitch was a compliment, and going to church was more important than being a Christian.

My mother was active in the Civil Rights Movement. Ironically, she fought against police brutality yet would beat us kids as if we were disobedient slaves. She was an advocate for fair housing while confining us to our rooms to maintain control, where life felt as small as the twin-sized bed that I shared with my sister. Mom also worked for voting rights, but seemed indifferent to our cries. Martin Luther King's "I Have a Dream" speech, espousing freedom and self-determination, was recognized in our house as the zenith of Black pride, while at the same time, my mother's harsh parenting practices remained routine and unquestioned. I don't recall being hugged or kissed, or feeling special as a child. What I remember most is how controlled I felt, and that I could not venture more than twenty-five feet from our house—the length of the concrete sidewalk that defined our front yard.

The most vivid war for me as a child was not the Vietnam War that was taking the lives of many young men I grew up with, or the

Watts riots that exploded in our immediate community. The most traumatic war for me was a war of emotions whose battleground was in my heart. The weapons were emotional neglect and physical abuse, and the enemy was my mother, whom I loved.

My silent mantra as a child was: *I can't wait to get out!* An older sister got pregnant and left home by the time she was fifteen. I followed her example, thinking more about my freedom than the responsibilities of raising a child. I denied any fear and was determined never to need my family again. After graduating from high school, I immediately took a secretarial job with the County of Los Angeles. When my father, a successful plumber, was shot to death by his girl-friend days before the Watts riots broke out, I don't recall feeling much emotion at his funeral. I can't say I knew him. I was seventeen and divorced. I don't think I even had a heart back then. I only remember how tightly I held my two-year-old son while our procession of cars was stopped several times by the National Guard as we carried my father's body across town to the cemetery.

In the loud silence of my surgical recuperation and in the years that followed, I realized that while I had physically walked away from the traumas of my childhood, I still carried them with me. The cruelties and disappointments were thriving, sheltered inside my body, mind, and heart. I did not know how to love and was too afraid to learn. I was beginning to acknowledge that I had spent most of my life running from unbearable pain and shame. Heart surgery had opened up not only my heart, but also my consciousness in such a way that my truth wouldn't leave me alone. I was awakened not only to how I had been harmed, but how I had harmed many people, including myself, and especially those I loved.

Prior to my heart surgery, I was unaware that I was *pregnant* with rage, that there was a rage child growing inside me who refused to be ignored and silenced. Open-heart surgery introduced me to rage by shocking me back into my terrified body. Surgery was only the tip of the iceberg, the beginning of a meltdown toward a deeper, more spiritual journey. Little did I know that my childhood mantra—*I can't wait to get out!*—was more than a mantra. It was my fate. I longed to live wide open, liberated from all forms of oppression, especially those that were self-imposed. It was during my recovery from heart surgery that I began to acknowledge that dancing with the heat of rage, my own and others, was not only my nature, but also my service.

Since that time, more than thirty years ago, I've realized a deeper awareness of rage and its wisdom. Along this journey, ancestors, elders, family members, therapy, world travel, and teachings from wisdom traditions have guided me. After years of what has been a soul-satisfying, magical, and, at times, difficult journey, I've come to understand my heart condition not only as an expression of unresolved and suppressed rage—some of which I inherited and maintained out of an unconscious loyalty to my family—but also as a sacred initiation into the riches of rage.

My journey revealed that rage deserved my attention and respect, and that I could not be fully emancipated until I healed my relationship with my parents, especially my mother. It wasn't enough to *know* I had suffered. I needed to return to that suffering, face it head-on with love, and leave it in the past where it belonged, before I could move forward and genuinely connect with other people and life itself. I recognized that I did not need to continue a legacy of hatred out of blind allegiance and block my chances to give and receive kindness.

I came to know intimately the roots of my parents' suffering— something I, too, carried and passed on to my son and others who dared to love me. I had more than an intellectual understanding of the love and challenges my parents endured raising us—I had a *felt* sense of it, and it was important for me to dignify not only my journey with rage, but also my parents'.

Gradually, I learned to forgive myself for not being able to change my past, but also for not being able to accept it. It took every ounce of my newly repaired heart to move from righteous rage to a more balanced truth. It was then that I could realize that my parents' suffering was not all that I had inherited. I had also inherited their prideful independence, ferocious determination, intelligence, a bias for justice, humor, music, and the ability to know and tell the truth. The pain of my past had undeniably and ironically contributed to tremendous strength and potential in my life, including the courage to write this book. Most importantly, I came to honor this journey as a life's work and service. I know in my bones the delicate power of being human— everyone has the capacity to hurt *and* love *and* heal.

Healing rage is *heart* work that requires courage and kindness, and many women, like me, seek guidance in reclaiming the positive energies that are distorted by the oppression of rage, and want to utilize the enormous power of rage as a vehicle for healing. This need led to the establishment of Bridges, Branches & Braids, an organization that began in 1992 for women to explore the pure character of rage through workshops, seminars, life coaching, and retreats. Through the Celebration of Rage™ retreat, women learn how to put rage in sacred perspective. We discover how we disguise rage, and are guided inward to deal directly with those aspects of ourselves that are unwanted. Through emotional release, art, ritual, and storytelling, we learn how to feed ourselves when our souls are starving. Women realize that the rage that feels larger than life—so intense that to face it we fear it might destroy us or someone else—is really the emotion of a small, hungry child, one that needs to be validated and nurtured. More profoundly, we discover that we are much more than the accumulation of events that have happened to us—we have full agency over our lives. We learn how to accept and forgive ourselves, and that we can heal through our own awareness without the permission, recognition, or approval of others, and be at peace in our own skin.

Women from many parts of the world have participated in the Celebration of Rage™ retreats, each completing detailed pre- and post-retreat questionnaires about their rage history, and each being personally interviewed. The collective insight from the lives of these courageous women contributes immeasurably to this book. At the same time, the cases presented in *Healing Rage* are fictionalized composites based on information shared during coaching sessions and retreats, as well as information from my own personal experiences. I have obtained the assistance of individuals to include helpful information about their experiences. Actual names and some key elements of the stories have been altered to maintain confidentiality and to honor the relationships we have forged in our work together. While *Healing Rage* is based on findings from women, its wisdom extends to, and equally benefits, male readers as well as young adults.

The basic assumption of *Healing Rage* is that unresolved rage from childhood trauma is still locked in our bodies and minds. This blocked energy manifests as *disguises of rage* in our adult lives—ways we cope with life while denying an intimate experience with living. These disguises become such an ingrained part of our existence that we forget that the origins are rage. While our disguises of rage attempt to protect us from the pain of our past, they more often re-create the past and perpetuate the very suffering we seek to avoid. Unresolved rage has been passed on from one generation to the next, contributing to rage inheritances that collectively plague the world, and each of us—whether we know it or not—is charged with transforming this legacy.

Our world is diminished by an ignorance and misuse of rage. Race and class oppression, conformity, greed, media violence, political corruption, indifference, war, abuse of the poor, abuse of the earth, and abuse of women and children are our society's ways of expressing rage, and we are our society. When we hate—any *one* or any *thing*—it is the same as stabbing ourselves in the heart. Regardless of our circumstances, however much we may deny, rationalize, or empathize with the traumatic conditions of our childhood and present lives, in every moment we have the power to feel, release, and transform rage, without harming others or ourselves. This work is not easy, just necessary!

You may have purchased this book because you realize that rage is interfering with your relationships and quality of life. Perhaps you are suffering a loss, or struggling with an illness. You may be seeking to understand an aspect of yourself that you are ashamed or frightened of. Understandably, you may be afraid of or bewildered by the rage that is all around you, and seek ways to turn within for refuge. Whatever the reasons, the fierce truth of rage is calling you to take a courageous step toward greater self-awareness, inner peace, and wholesome service.

The title *Healing Rage* was chosen with careful consideration. For some people, *healing* implies that something is wrong that needs to be right. Here, the word is used more to point toward a need for sacred attention and intention. In this work, healing is about remembering who we are and what we deeply know. It is about learning how to work with our minds in ways that relieve suffering. Healing is also about cultivating a tolerance for peaceful liberation. This means allowing the discomfort often associated with rage to inform us for the benefit of a healthier life and future, and it may even mean that we give up a bit of comfort for more consciousness.

The process of *Healing Rage* is not a quick fix, nor is it an attempt to eliminate rage from our lives. Rage isn't going away. We will continue to be triggered by conditions that give rise to it. These conditions are both outside and within us. Rather, this is a journey of profound introspection that allows our most enraging and shame-provoking experiences to heal us.

Healing Rage is an invitation to wild awakenings and deep beauty. When we embrace this truth, we reveal fully to ourselves, and to the world, our exquisiteness and infinite potential. Let us begin—bring your own light, and a mirror!

PART ONE

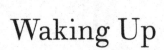

Waking Up

1

The Birth of Rage

Rage is an oppressed *child* emotion housed deep within our bodies, minds, and spirits. Throughout this book, I will refer to her as our inner *Rage Child*. We tend to react to our rage child as an emotional enemy to be eliminated, a fire to be feared. More accurately, our rage child is a natural resource of misused energy, and she exists whether we acknowledge her or not. She is the daughter of our traumas, the twin of our shame, the burden of our denied histories, the foreign language of our emotional pain, and the wisdom that helps us heal.

Our rage child is at once a young and old emotion: *young* because she is tied to our personal childhood traumas that have been suppressed; *old* because she is an accumulation of unresolved anger and shame, some of which has been passed on for many generations. Few of us realize how much rage we have and how rage controls our lives. We feel trapped in a revolving door of conflicting emotions—victims of our own and others' rage, yet socialized to be ashamed of our natural response to it. Sadly, we tend to turn rage inward, against ourselves. We fail to understand that the ongoing, often subconscious struggle to repress rage causes suffering and drains our life force. *Whether we are ignorant or aware does not change the fierce truth that most of us are enraged—with good reason—and the fires of rage continue to burn within us with or without our acknowledgment or permission.*

RAGE, NOT ANGER

Rage and anger are often regarded as the same emotion, but they are distinct experiences. Anger is primarily associated with a current injustice, dislike, or disappointment—a driver cutting in front of you without signaling, a disagreement at work, annoyance at a clerk who forgot to give you correct change, an argument over who said what. We have some control over what we are experiencing, and some ability to leave the situation or create a more desirable outcome.

Rage is an accumulation of anger, an experience that is primarily physical and rooted to unresolved or unknown traumas that shamed us in childhood. Rage is a visceral and instinctive response when we feel we have little or no control over what is threatening or harming us.

When we are enraged our experience is *beyond* anger and rarely brings healing relief. We will discover in the following chapters that anger (referred to as *Defiance*) is one of six disguises of rage. Many of us do not act out or show our rage and anger. These are feelings that we experience within, at times may express outwardly, but more commonly hide or deny. Over time, we become capable of hiding our experiences of rage and anger from others, and even from ourselves.

TRAUMA GIVES BIRTH TO RAGE

Trauma gives birth to rage—an experience of severe emotional shock that causes substantial and lasting damage to our psychological well-being. Trauma is experienced as being intensely overwhelmed by a perceived threat or actual harm. Trauma can be a single incident of devastating loss, violation, or injury, or a chronic atmosphere of fear and neglect.

The traumas that give birth to rage typically occur in our families between the ages of birth and twelve years of age. This birth takes place within our mind and body and significantly influences the rest of our lives. As children, we are often not immediately aware of our experiences of rage but are more likely to feel confused, frightened, and hurt. Rage, naturally born in the face of trauma, becomes problematic when our vulnerability goes unaddressed, and it has a cumulative effect on our development as we grow older. While traumatic experiences give birth to rage, it's not the trauma that devastates us most profoundly as children. *Rather, it's the ways in which our traumatic experiences are responded to that have the most enraging and lasting impact.*

The following are several types of traumas that give birth to rage in childhood: *emotional neglect, emotional abuse, verbal abuse, loss,* and *physical violence and sexual abuse.* Read through them and notice which ones resemble your childhood experiences.

Emotional Neglect

Many of us discover that we are enraged because we did not feel loved *enough* as children. We came from an environment in which there was food and shelter, clothing, even toys, sometimes two parents, a house, and a dog, *but . . .* Emotional neglect results from experiences where parents and other authority figures were gravely unresponsive, or there was a lack of priority or awareness of our emotional needs. The trauma of emotional neglect occurred when there was a chronic atmosphere in which:

• You felt ignored or invisible—not seen, heard, or valued.
• Your parents were unavailable or there were broken promises.

- There was an absence of touch and tenderness.
- You were given things instead of time and attention.
- You were talked at, not talked to, or not made to understand things.
- You were treated as if you didn't (or shouldn't) have needs beyond what was provided.
- You were responsible for parenting your siblings and/or your parents.
- You were attended to only if you were ill.
- You felt something was wrong but no one would talk about it.
- You spent significant time hoping, longing, or wishing things could be different.
- You felt unwanted.

Sadly, these seemingly *normal* examples of neglect are nevertheless traumatizing, and they contribute to children growing into angry and guilty adults. Lizbeth shares her experience of emotional neglect in this way:

> I was able to piece together the story of my birth from distant relatives. Apparently, when my mother was pregnant with me, my father had also impregnated his girlfriend, a woman he loved and wanted to marry. But my mother would not divorce him. While my mother was in labor with me, my father was with his girlfriend who was also in labor, but she died giving birth to a stillborn child. I imagine my father was grief-stricken from this loss—a loss I feel I always shared. He was unhappy and made everyone else unhappy. He always acted like he hated my face and he had nothing to do with me. I guess I reminded him of how stuck he felt with my mother and me, and the child and love of his life he lost. It didn't help that I looked just like my father, something my mother always reminded me of. Neither my mother nor father ever talked about this but I knew—I could feel that I was unwanted.

When we come from emotionally neglectful families, we often feel guilty about our feelings. We live with doubt and shame, and cannot understand why we feel empty, unlovable, and unloving.

Emotional Abuse

An atmosphere of chronic fear and anxiety resulting from emotional abuse and violation of boundaries is perhaps the most common form of childhood trauma reported by women. Frequent situations include:

- Your parents withheld loving emotions to distance themselves from you or punish you.
- You were taught to hate or belittle races, economic classes, ethnicities, cultures, genders, and others who were not like you.
- You were distrusted and questioned—there was an automatic assumption that you had done something wrong.
- You were treated as an object of service to authorities.
- You were praised for or expected to do things you felt incapable of doing.
- You were humiliated if you made a mistake, didn't have the answer, or didn't measure up.
- You were smothered, overpowered, or overcontrolled.
- You were praised more for what you did instead of who you were.
- You could not have your own dreams, restricted from what you passionately felt or desired.
- You were expected to tell all, show all, and prove all.
- You witnessed someone you loved be abused or violated and were unable or too frightened to stop it.
- You felt confused and received conflicting messages—*Make sure your sister doesn't fall* but *don't touch her.* Or I *hate your father,* and *you look just like him.*

- You could not show any intense emotions or naturally express your feelings without being silenced or punished.
- You were socially isolated.
- One or both of your parents were jealous of you.
- You had to be the caretaker of your parents' moods, emotions, or well-being.

Emotional abuse is by far the most common and pervasive form of abuse that gives birth to rage. Sheryl experienced emotional abuse from the age of eight to twelve, a stage in which she was challenged with defining her self-worth:

> Mom always talked about not wanting to live and she would threaten to kill herself whenever we got into an argument. I would get home from school and she would be passed out on the couch and my first thought was that she had killed herself. I spent a lot of time worrying about how she might kill herself. I didn't know whether to feel mad or sad. And I couldn't tell anybody. I feared for a long time that my anger would be the cause of her death.

Emotional abuse leaves us angry, helpless, and hopeless. We distrust others and our own value as people.

Verbal Abuse

Verbal abuse is a form of emotional abuse that involves a deliberately hostile intention. Verbal abuse creates an atmosphere of cruelty and fear that corrodes self-worth. You know you were verbally abused if you were given these kinds of messages:

- You're nothing.
- You're worthless.
- You're stupid.
- You're fat.

- You're black.
- You're skinny.
- You're ugly.
- Get out of my face.
- I should have aborted you.
- You're always fucking up.
- Something is wrong with you.
- You can't do anything right.
- You're a bitch, just like your mother.
- I'm gonna kick your ass.
- Shut up.
- I'll kill you.
- I brought you into this world and I will take you out.
- I hate it when you act just like your father. I got rid of him and I will get rid of you.

When we are verbally abused or live in a climate of intense dislike as children, we are ashamed of existing. We question our worth, and we feel disinterested in caring for others and ourselves. We feel helpless and powerless in our lives, both ashamed and enraged, and don't see why anyone would love us.

Loss

Other incidents of shock and emotional trauma include the loss of love and loved ones to death, divorce, betrayal, or abandonment. These can include:

- You lost your parents or your parents died.
- You experienced the death of a significant caretaker or sibling.
- Your parents separated or divorced.
- You witnessed or felt responsible for the death of someone.
- You felt betrayed or abandoned by a care provider.
- You lost an animal, friend, home, limb, or item of significant

value through death, illogical and unexpected removal, destruction, or disappearance.
- Your family moved around often and you lost friends or felt unsure of yourself, constantly having to adjust to new situations.
- Something terrible happened that you could not stop or control.
- You had to live with a prolonged or terminal illness.

Mildred shares a childhood experience when she emotionally lost her father:

> My father absolutely adored me until I reached puberty. He accidentally walked in on me in the bathroom and I was nude. I was twelve and I'll never forget the shock on his face. From then on I felt completely abandoned by him. He no longer held me, talked to me, or played with me. I would scream at him trying to understand what happened, and he would just leave the room. The cost I paid to become a young woman was the loss of my father. I was confused by his release of me and to this day I long to sit on his lap and laugh again.

When we can't understand the loss of what we desperately rely on, we naturally feel abandoned, hurt, confused, and angry. We learn to distrust love. We feel lost and struggle to make sense of our world.

Physical Violence and Sexual Abuse

Physical violence and sexual abuse toward children are all too common traumatic experiences that give rise to rage. This form of abuse is a bodily violation of extreme humiliation and devastation. It is a precursor to long-lasting issues that profoundly affect our relationship to power in others and within ourselves. You suffered physical violence and sexual abuse if:

- You were beaten, slapped, or shoved by your parents, guardians, and others who were older or had more control.

- You felt sexually obligated or forced through rape, incest, or molestation.
- You were sexually or physically violated by someone known or unknown outside of your family.
- You were emotionally raped, forced to tolerate sexual language, pornography, or to witness sexual activity.
- You felt you needed to respond sexually or violently to be loved.
- You felt physically or sexually vulnerable due to poor boundaries or a lack of protection.

When we are physically or sexually abused as children by those we love, trust, or rely on, we carry a shame so deep in our bones that it silences our voices, numbs our bodies, warps our thinking, and closes our hearts, sometimes for a lifetime. Vanessa shares her experience of incest as a child:

> I had to manipulate my mind into believing I didn't hurt. I wanted to tell but I didn't want to get in trouble, and I didn't want my Mom and Dad to argue. I was also afraid of what my friends would say or what anyone would say if the word got out. I was terrified of my Dad. He told me he loved me but he also told me he would hurt me if I told. I kept it a secret to protect my Mom and the family. When I finally did tell my Mom, her response was: You have ruined my life and this family! How could you do this to me? That was the day I lost my Mom, my family, and everything that mattered. Now he has my Mom and they are a family, and I have nothing.

When we are physically and sexually abused, we distrust our instincts and we especially distrust loved ones. We feel damaged, torn from the truth we embody and terrified to reclaim it. Life feels unsafe, and intimacy is both longed for and feared.

FROM RAGE CHILD TO RAGE WOMAN

When we are taught or forced to deny what we feel while traumatic things are happening in childhood, we grow into troubled adolescents facing problems that childhood did not prepare us for. We are more likely to distrust others, doubt ourselves, and feel guilty and inferior—all of which we must attempt to hide.

As a teenager, the emphasis is on becoming an adult—too often becoming something or somebody else. Often we are told how to think and feel instead of how to discover who we are. For many of us, we enter an oppressive and hostile world of inadequate education, economic hardships, quick-to-jail programs, drugs, sensationalism of violence in the mass media, and a pervasive atmosphere of disrespect and high control. Then we are expected to act like responsible adults. Some of us try, but understandably, we often fall short. We begin to experience failure all around us—within and outside of our families.

As teenagers, we are often thought of as lazy, crazy, and disobedient. But it is closer to the truth that we are afraid of the speed and greed in our lives—afraid that we can't keep up. The adults in our world seem overwhelmed in the face of our disguised pain and helplessness. Ashamed of our hidden inadequacy, we rebel, often caving to the temptations of drugs, sex, and rock and roll—*and* alcohol abuse, teenage pregnancy, suicide, homicide, and depression.

Many of us struggle with body image and sexuality, and an intense need to belong. Pressure to be sexual can make it difficult to choose to be simply touched and hugged. Our reactions to peers can range from feeling shut down and depressed to being overly sexual. While this is true for many of us during adolescence, those of us who have been physically and sexually abused will often cave to sexual pressure to belong, when it is physical and emotional intimacy that we long for.

As we enter adulthood, challenged with complexities of intimacy, sexuality, work, family, and partnerships, life can feel like a chronic, low-level threat. We feel things we don't understand, say things we don't feel, and do things we don't mean to do. Our fear and shame become even more exaggerated when we feel isolated, confused, or threatened. We often avoid our feelings because *feeling* is dangerous—providing a faceless reminder of our inability to be safe and stay in control. There is a frightening instinct operating within us that we don't trust or comprehend. Oddly, we often find ourselves in situations similar to those of our early childhood, wondering why they seem to repeat themselves again and again in our lives.

Some of us become parents to flesh-and-blood children who are forced to share emotional space with an unacknowledged sibling—our denied rage child. As mothers and oftentimes the heads of households, the family is where we commonly control and reenact unresolved rage. Predictably and often innocently, we traumatize our children, by passing on these messages:

- Make me proud.
- Never disappoint me.
- You should be grateful.
- You have it better than I did.
- Always be happy and polite.
- Never show anger.
- Never embarrass me.
- Never disagree with me.
- Never make me angry.
- Always put me first.
- Never be afraid or never show fear.

Sadly, when we become parents without an awareness of our own personal rage, we tend to re-create the same traumas we experienced as children, thus giving birth to another generation of rage. We pass on our legacy of abuse while disowning the pain and shame of our rage child.

Childhood trauma is not the only disturbance associated with rage. Certainly there are social, environmental, and political traumas—past and present—that surround us and profoundly affect our lives, yet our programmed response to trauma and to rage is well established by the time we reach young adulthood. We often discover as adults that it is easier if not more satisfying to fight social, environmental, and political battles than to face up to the shame-filled, deeper roots of childhood rage.

In our adult lives, we often search for ways to tell the truth about what happened in childhood, but even as adults, we distrust or deny our experiences and fear the consequences. Unknowingly, we continue to traumatize ourselves by re-creating the scenes that harmed us. We inherited this dilemma from people we loved and trusted, and, while it secretly shames and haunts us, it was and still is what we know best and what we do out of an unconscious loyalty to our parents and ancestors. Despite our painful journeys, many of us succeed materially. However, success is not to be confused with healing.

OUR RAGE INHERITANCE

We usually think of our rage as belonging exclusively to us, yet you may have thought, in the heat of an enraging encounter: *Hmm . . . what I'm feeling right now seems larger, louder, and older than the present situation!* The truth of the matter is that all of us are part of a much larger tapestry of familial and ancestral rage. We are all recipients of a rage inheritance.

A rage inheritance is a bequest of unresolved rage from our parents and ancestors. This includes generations of unresolved rage from institutions of influence, such as the family, law, politics, education, and religion, as well as from social constructions such as ethnicity, race, class, gender, and culture.

One way to understand our rage inheritance is through the laws of cause and effect, which state that nothing exists on its own, everything has come from earlier circumstances. For example, we each are alive because our parents met at an earlier time. We did not just appear, nor do we exist without a long lineage. As infants, we learned by imitation. We mirrored and reacted to our parents, as our parents learned from theirs, in an unbroken line of unconscious loyalty.

Particular patterns of fear, shame, and rage are taught by one generation and passed to the next. Like it or not, our parents and ancestors are with us even when we don't know them, don't like them, or don't remember them. Many of the ways we are and the things we do reflect this inheritance, including our appearance, gestures, talents, movements, habits—and the ways in which we relate to rage.

Whatever our parents and ancestors could not or would not resolve is gifted to us to transform—this is our karmic reality and our challenge. We are usually unaware of our rage inheritance. Shame, secrecy, and complicity serve to obscure and more deeply embed these patterns. We innocently embody the unresolved generational rage and pass it on to the next generation. When our rage inheritance is unknown or ignored, we subconsciously collude in contributing to a society of ignorance, war, greed, indifference, hatred, violence, and abuse. This recycling of rage continues until we can heal the traumas that caused them.

BELOVED IS THE RAGE CHILD

One story that profoundly illuminates generational rage is the Pulitzer Prize–winning novel *Beloved*, by Toni Morrison. Inspired by an article about a runaway slave, Margaret Garner, Morrison tells a complex and poetic story of motherly love expressed through child murder. The novel's main character, Sethe, has endured a life of brutality and pain at the hands of white slave owners. She kills her own infant daughter, slitting the baby's throat, to prevent her from being stolen and raised as a slave. Years later her daughter reappears as a ghost spirit—Beloved. Sethe's entire life is altered as she becomes obsessed with being forgiven and loses herself in Beloved's insatiable hunger and rage. Beloved's anguish is expressed in two questions: *Why'd you hurt me? Why'd you leave me?* Sethe's sincere response: *It wasn't like that child. I loved you. I always loved you, baby!*

A child does not understand the tough choices a mother must sometimes make, nor can a child comprehend how any harm could be a gesture of love. In a child's mind, it simply means *you don't love me.*

Many of us were confused by mixed messages of childhood love and harm and were forced to silence (or kill) our rage in order to survive. But this rage never leaves us despite our best efforts. Like Beloved, we want to ask our mothers, parents, or guardians—*Why did you hurt me? Why did you leave me?* Our ancestors had these questions, our children have these questions, and most importantly, our rage child is asking us these questions.

We may or may not have visible whip marks on our back like Sethe, or scars on our necks like Beloved, but we have all been scarred, and we have all scarred others. And we all have ways of ensuring that harm never befalls us again, even if it means hurting others and ourselves. The pain and hurt that created our rage are desperately searching for liberation.

How do we help our inner rage child—our Beloved—understand the choices we have made to survive? How do we help her comprehend that our most horrible acts were the best choices we knew to make at the time? How do we forgive ourselves for harming ourselves, and for the shame, fear, and self-hatred we have swallowed from our past?

We begin to heal rage when we discover within ourselves that we are all like Sethe—women who have had to make difficult choices, *and* had mothers, fathers, guardians, and ancestors who harmed and loved us. As mothers and women, our pasts haunt us, and at times we feel unlovable and unforgivable. We are all akin to Beloved—we embody a rage child that we have killed, silenced, misused, neglected, or abandoned, a child spirit within that demands answers. We are all like Sethe's other children who were traumatized by their sister's murder—terrified children in adult bodies, ashamed to be seen or helped, running away from love because we are afraid it will kill us. We are all like Sethe's lover, Paul D—starving for love yet overcome by temptation. We are all like the slave hunters—ignorant of our self-serving pursuits and entitlements and unaware of the pain we cause others and ourselves. And we are all like the community of women who comforted and sustained Sethe—despite our pain we are capable of inspiring and transforming others and ourselves.

Rage is inevitable. No matter what we do, our hearts will break and we will hurt others and be hurt time and time again. Healing invites us to honor our beloved rage child as that part of us that is in pain and in need of our kind attention and care.

2

Into Rage, Out of Body

THE BODY/MIND SPLIT

When we experience trauma in childhood, our minds can't make sense of what is occurring. Because we are emotionally underdeveloped, the body absorbs the full blow of our trauma. As a result the body becomes a dreadful war zone that we must escape in order to cope with the intolerable pain we feel. Because we are children, we cannot physically escape, but we can attempt to escape mentally by a psychological process known as *splitting*. Splitting protects us from remembering and experiencing our traumas. It is a necessary psychological defense when, for example, we love and are dependent on those who abuse us. Denise, suffering from physical abuse and emotional neglect, shares:

> I remember when I was about six years old, my father beat me
> and a few hours later, took me out for ice cream, acting as
> though nothing had happened. Things like this happened a

lot. Sometimes I'd have obvious bruises on my face and arms. People would frown at us and I felt odd, embarrassed, and special at the same time.

A child's confusion when she loves her abuser is in itself traumatic, forcing a split between body and mind. Denise's bafflement does not mean that rage was not felt; it means that love was felt more. In that moment of innocence, rage was not conscious or immediately accessible. Denise knew her father must love her and ice cream was proof of his love. She grew to conclude that love included beatings.

When we are both loved and abused by our guardians, we become confused and learn to distrust what we feel. Because we are dependent on their care, we accept their reality over our own and grow doubtful of what we deeply know to be true.

When our minds and bodies split in the face of trauma, like Denise we separate the feelings in our body from the thoughts in our minds. When we split in this way, the release of rage is interrupted and becomes trapped in the body as we take our minds elsewhere— to a safer place.

Since the onset of our traumas, our body has contained and concealed the pain of rage. We move through our adult lives unaware that we are pregnant with rage. It's as if there were a rowdy party occurring inside our body. Granted, every now and then we might smell a bit of marijuana, or stumble over a few empty liquor bottles, notice that the car has new dents, or that there are clothes lying around that don't belong to us. But we don't *think* much about it and we don't *feel* any of it. Anyone or anything that threatens to put us in contact with this pain is avoided or discounted. We convince ourselves that there's no problem, but the body knows otherwise, and eventually the evidence of our rage bleeds through our mind's defenses.

The body/mind split can be most painful and confusing in matters of intimacy. Intimacy threatens to reveal what we attempt to hide, so we avoid it. Our body has a keen recollection of any physical or emotional trauma suffered at the hands of a loved one. When our early experiences of touch are associated with trauma, we become frightened and ashamed. We find ourselves both avoiding and craving touch. Either way, fear is blocking the intimacy we crave and deserve.

The split can be readily observed in situations where women tolerate physical and sexual abuse at the hands of a loved one for long periods of time. In many of these relationships, the body seeks physical intimacy but settles for abuse, while the mind makes excuses for our situation. The irony is that abuse can be the closest we've ever come to intimacy. These contacts are not intimate, but rather painful and shaming, yet they awaken us to older memories of love. Abuse also forces us to feel, and temporarily reassures us that we live in a body. Over time, physical needs become distorted, boundaries blurred, and abuse from others and ourselves becomes normal—something we cannot live with or without. We don't realize that these are reenactments of childhood trauma that keep our mind and body separate.

Many of us react to the body/mind split by becoming obsessed with how we look, correcting imperfections that no one else sees, while others hide their bodies, fearing intense discomfort from unwanted outside attention. The bottom line is that too many of us don't like what we see when we look at ourselves and hope the pain we feel never shows. Some of us do like what we see but don't feel who we are.

When touch is what has traumatized us in our early years, many of us avoid touching ourselves, or even taking a good look at our own bodies. For example, thousands die each year from breast cancer because we avoid breast self-examination. We miss out on the wisdom our bodies bestow.

We all crave the intimacy of touch—tender contact—but many are confused about the differences between physical and sexual intimacy. Consider, for example, the sexual hunger of many teenage girls. People are quick to label such behavior as sexual addiction when it is more often a longing for tenderness. Somewhere along the way, we have learned that sex is what you do when you want contact. Therefore, we feed our bodies sex, which leaves us only temporarily satisfied because our deeper yearning is for something much more intimate.

The body/mind split is further culturally sanctioned when society benefits from our woundedness. Often, more value is placed on those whom our bodies please than on who we are as human beings. Consider the profits of prostitution and the oppressive commercialization of our bodies as entertainment, titillation, and targets of violence. In some cultures, women are punished or even killed for exposing skin, and female genital mutilation is considered a condition of survival and social acceptance. When we are objectified in this way, we split body and mind in order to survive—mentally focusing on one reality while our bodies are experiencing another.

The body/mind split plays a crucial role in our lives as long as we are ashamed of our wholeness, and understandably, we often are. In fact, we are willing to do just about anything to avoid reexperiencing the shame of childhood traumas.

THE RAGE/SHAME DUO

Just as mothers have a psychological bond with their children, rage has a psychological bond with shame—its twin emotion. What makes rage such a volatile emotion is its kinship with shame. While we looked to our mothers for protection, shame looks to her sister emotion, rage, for protection, and vice versa.

Rage and shame are locked in a complicated, symbiotic struggle. Like many twins, rage and shame are mistaken for each other, and, like many siblings, they compete to have their conflicting needs met. For example, rage wants freedom to tell the truth, while shame wants protection and safety. Shame wants to hide, collapse, retreat, and surrender in the face of conflict, while rage wants to fight, force, and persist. Rage wants to stay awake and alert, while shame would prefer to be asleep and sluggish.

Rage and shame incite each other—when one is active, it invariably triggers the other. When rage becomes activated, for example, we can lose control and overexpose ourselves. Being exposed can make us feel vulnerable and ashamed. The vulnerability of this shame in turn incites a protective storm of rage. Here's how Phyllis experienced it:

> An important project at work was not going my way and I was so enraged about it, I had to get out of there. I took a walk to a nearby mall. While admiring a well-dressed mannequin in the window, I noticed my face reflected in the glass. I saw myself as wounded—frightened, vulnerable, and vulgar. I felt embarrassed and horrified. The next thing I knew, I was in the store and within one hour, had charged my credit card up into the thousands. Later I was enraged that I had, once again, put myself in debt.

Phyllis initially felt rage but saw shame reflected in the glass window. Her shame was intolerable, so her righteous rage provided a needed excuse for Phyllis to purchase enough clothing to cover the shame she was attempting to deny. Later feeling guilty, she became enraged toward her own guilt. Phyllis reminds us that rage and shame trigger each other in an incessant duo.

Another result of the Rage/Shame Duo is a subconscious process known as *projecting* (discussed further in the "Solving Rage Riddles" chapter). Here we give over an unwanted part of ourselves to another without that person's knowledge (or our own). That person, in our mind, lives out this unwanted part, which in turn provides a continuing target for our projection of rage. Joyce shares it well:

> I've been dating Paul for four years and his life is a mess. He can never get his act together and his world is chaotic. I go crazy around him. If I didn't tell him what to do, he wouldn't know, and he'd drag us both down the tubes. I know I'm critical of him but he's such a child. Why do I have him in my life? Why can't I seem to stop tormenting myself over how he is? And why is it that everyone I get close to is like this?

Upon further exploration, Joyce realized that her biggest fear is returning to the chaotic world of her childhood, where anytime she made a mess she was verbally or physically abused. Joyce's adult world is one in which she controls things so tightly that nothing is ever out of place. Determined not to feel shame, Joyce becomes her raging parent abusing her partner as she was abused in childhood. Paul, unknowingly, represents the chaotic and shaming world of her childhood—a world Joyce cannot leave behind. When Joyce is projecting her shame onto Paul, she is relinquishing her responsibility and her power to transform her own emotional pain pattern.

Our intertwined experiences of rage and shame represent a complex emotional language. For some women, it is safer to feel rage than shame. For others, it is safer to feel shame than rage. But for too many, it is never safe *enough* to feel. For this reason, we wear disguises of rage.

PART TWO

The Six Disguises
of Rage

3

Determining Your
Disguises of Rage

Many of us go through our lives maintaining a good front. We may have all of the trappings—good job, higher education, and material gain, yet we have an inherent discontent with our lives that won't go away. We manage to look okay from the outside, hiding those periods of despair when we feel everything caving in on us by keeping to ourselves. We express confidence on the surface and feel fear or dread underneath. We know we feel chaotic and on the edge, but we hide it, sometimes beautifully, even from ourselves. This is accomplished by wearing disguises of rage.

Disguises are our rage child's armor—the coats we wear year round to cope with the chill of life, even on a warm day. They are our ways to be in control of a chronically frightening life. Disguises keep our body and mind experiences split so that we can manage the intolerable threat of shame that may awaken traumatic childhood memories. Disguises also serve as symbolic templates of older stories of rage that require our attention. These templates were established during childhood and continue into our adult lives with slight modifications until we transform them. They have played a significant role in our survival but they interfere with our healing. We continue to wear our disguises because we perceive these obscure expressions of rage as being safer and more acceptable than truth itself.

DETERMINING YOUR DISGUISES OF RAGE

To determine your disguises of rage, select from the following statements those that most commonly represent your life pattern or instinctive response to the world. Avoid selecting statements that may reflect actions you have taken only occasionally, and choose instead those that are your typical life pattern, thought, or tendency—even if you do them less and less.

For example: Esther blew up at a salesperson who flirted with her when she was purchasing a car. This action could be characteristic of Statement #31: *I have a quick temper*. However, this action was new for Esther, not a life pattern. What is more characteristic of a life pattern for Esther is Statement #28: *I have difficulty setting boundaries and asking for what I want*. For Esther, Statement #28 would be an appropriate selection.

Take your time and read through all of the statements before making your selections. For each statement, place an X in the appropriate column: *Yes, this has been a lifelong belief or tendency!* or *No, this has not been a lifelong belief or tendency!*

SELF-ASSESSMENT

Characteristics of Disguises of Rage	Yes, this has been a lifelong belief or tendency!	No, this has not been a lifelong belief or tendency!
1. I am vindictive toward others who cross me.		
2. I become incapacitated, speechless, or feel small in the face of disapproval or anger.		
3. I do only what is required and resent additional expectations others have of me.		
4. I do everything I can to keep others from becoming upset.		
5. I overindulge and live beyond my means.		
6. I am unaware of being afraid.		
7. I become angry with others when I feel hurt, disappointed, or need time to myself.		
8. I doubt myself and hope others will take care of my emotional and financial needs.		
9. In general, I feel emotionally heavy, hopeless, and cynical.		
10. I feel intense frustration when I can't do anything to pull someone out of sadness or depression.		
11. I find it difficult to rest, be still, be quiet, or do nothing.		
12. Others accuse me of being bossy, insensitive, self-righteous, and selfish.		
13. I believe that most powers-that-be are inadequate and fall short of my expectations, and must pay for what they have done or not done.		

Characteristics of Disguises of Rage	Yes, this has been a lifelong belief or tendency!	No, this has not been a lifelong belief or tendency!
14. I expect that exceptions will be made for my hard luck.		
15. I isolate or distance myself from others to avoid talking or having to engage in day-to-day life.		
16. I must take care of others first, and if there is time left over, I will care for myself. I feel like I must sneak time to care for myself.		
17. I generally feel hungry for more (time, money, fun, knowledge, sleep, chocolates, etc.).		
18. I must take charge of people, places, and situations or else things will get screwed up.		
19. I believe that most rules restrict my life.		
20. In conflict, I become confused and find it hard to know what I want.		
21. I feel unable to exert energy toward what is important to my health and well-being.		
22. I give so that others will not be upset. If others are upset it is because of something I've done or not done.		
23. I overwork, spend, drink, drug, eat, sex, TV, etc.		
24. I generally feel entitled to express my anger toward others.		
25. I feel I must fight to protect myself or others will take advantage of me.		
26. I often feel inadequate and unqualified.		

Characteristics of Disguises of Rage	Yes, this has been a lifelong belief or tendency!	No, this has not been a lifelong belief or tendency!
27. I routinely question the purpose or point of my life.		
28. I have difficulty setting boundaries and asking for what I want.		
29. I put myself at financial risk by gambling, spending, rushing, or investing.		
30. When challenged or confronted, I become demanding, critical, and judgmental.		
31. I have a quick temper.		
32. I have a history of financial insufficiency or instability.		
33. I over-relate or identify with my pain, illness, and despair.		
34. I pretend to be perfect and positive no matter what is happening.		
35. I take on more than I can handle, then resent the weight of my responsibilities.		
36. When others disappoint me, I can appear heartless and often will distance or leave (the job, relationship, friendship, etc.).		

There are three types of disguises, which we will discuss at length in the next chapters, each comprising two disguises of rage:

- Fight Types—*Dominance* and *Defiance*
- Flight Types—*Distraction* and *Devotion*
- Shrink Types—*Dependence* and *Depression*

Typically we have one, maybe two predominant disguises of rage that we established in childhood with overlapping traits from the other disguises. To determine your primary disguises of rage, transfer the statement numbers you marked in the first or "Yes" column to the matrix below. Total each column in the matrix. Your total in any given column can range from 0–6. Your higher numbers will most likely represent your disguises of rage.

Defiance	Dependence	Depression	Devotion	Distraction	Dominance
1	2	3	4	5	6
7	8	9	10	11	12
13	14	15	16	17	18
19	20	21	22	23	24
25	26	27	28	29	30
31	32	33	34	35	36
Totals	Totals	Totals	Totals	Totals	Totals

A shortcut for determining your primary disguises of rage is to reflect on how you went about completing this exercise. For example, you probably wear a *Devotion* disguise if you found yourself saying: *I'm all of them depending on the situation!* You are likely to wear *Defiance* if you were thinking: *Why should I put myself in one or two categories? You're not the boss of me!* If you checked "Yes" to most of the statements other than the *Dependence* statements, you lean in the direction of wearing the *Dependence* disguise. You have tendencies of *Distraction* if you didn't bother with the task and instead fast-forwarded to the next section of the book. If you just didn't feel up to the task, you may wear the *Depression* disguise. And you are sure to wear *Dominance* if you skimmed the questions and found that most of them didn't apply to you, and in fact was a waste of your time. If you fall into more than two of the disguises, that's okay, too! It does not matter—what matters is that you keep reading!

There is yet another way to determine your disguises of rage. Give the assessment to two or three loved ones or close friends and ask them to complete it for you. There is one catch: You must promise to continue to be their friend even if you don't like what they see or say. Relationships have been known to deepen when friends complete the assessment for each other.

HIGH-CONTROL AND OUT-OF-CONTROL TYPES

Disguises of rage can further be understood when placed along the dimension of high control and out of control. The *High-Control and Out-of-Control* range has to do with how certain disguise clusters relate to anger, guilt, and shame. Refer to your Disguises of Rage Self-Assessment scores to determine where you are located on the spectrum of *High Control and Out of Control*.

High-Control Types

DOMINANCE, DEVOTION, AND DEPRESSION
Those of us who wear the *Dominance* and *Devotion* disguises share high control in our effort to conquer and escape. We need to be needed by others, we know what's best for them, and we need to clone others in our image. We are focused, perfectionists, and generally faultless. *Dominance* and *Devotion* disguises have different experiences of shame. The *Dominance* disguise tends to experience more rage than shame, whereas the *Devotion* disguise tends to experience more shame than rage.

The third high-control disguise, *Depression*, seeks control by forcing others to rescue us and provide us with energy. The *Depression* disguise's control is less verbal and more concealed, but nonetheless communicated, i.e., through withdrawal, silence, or suicide attempts or thoughts. *Depression* and *Dominance* share withdrawal as a form of control, whereas *Devotion* is more likely to control by holding tightly to others.

Out-of-Control Types

DEFIANCE, DISTRACTION, AND DEPENDENCE

The *Defiance, Distraction,* and *Dependence* disguises share the characteristics of being impulsive, entitled, and insatiable. We want immediate gratification and approval from others. Others owe us their undivided attention! We can be self-indulgent saboteurs. What distinguishes us out-of-control types is our experience of shame. Those who wear the *Defiance* and *Distraction* disguises are likely to experience more rage than shame and feel others are at fault, whereas people who wear the *Dependence* disguise feel guilty and resentful for not being in control, and are likely to experience more shame.

SHADOW DISGUISES

Disguises of rage are distortions of reality, extremes that have opposing forces that are feared, avoided, desired, and ultimately realized. Consider them shadow disguises—those aspects of ourselves that we dislike in others but are hidden or even denied parts of ourselves. For example, each *high-control* disguise has an *out-of-control* disguise as its shadow that it avoids experiencing, yet relies upon to navigate events in the world, and the reverse is also true, as indicated by this chart:

High Control	Out of Control
Dominance avoids experiencing Dependence	Dependence avoids experiencing Dominance
Devotion avoids experiencing Defiance	Defiance avoids experiencing Devotion
Depression avoids experiencing Distraction	Distraction avoids experiencing Depression

For example, *Dominance* is terrified of becoming dependent, while *Dependence* avoids taking control of her own life. *Devotion* cannot tolerate the harshness of *Defiance*, while *Defiance* believes that pleasing others is manipulative and violates freedom. *Depression* finds herself paralyzed in the speed of distraction, while *Distraction* dreads the stillness of *Depression*.

As with any extreme, we inevitably find ourselves on the other side of something equally painful and terrifying. This dynamic becomes even more complex when we consider that we wear more than one disguise of rage, or more mind-boggling when we understand that we wear many of them.

The following chapters and descriptions of disguises of rage are not intended to simplify or categorize our complex lives. Rather they are attempts to reveal our deceptions of rage and invite us to reexamine what might ordinarily be considered normal or justified behavior.

4

Fight Types—
In the Ring with Rage

Dominance and *Defiance*—at a Glance

Fight types lead with anger when we feel attacked, trapped, or caught off guard. We have high control needs, readily confront conflict, pretend to be unafraid, deny or ignore shame, and feel faultless—*Somebody must pay!* We seek justice and reprisal, and would say that what we do *is for your own good!* Fight types become angry to divert the embarrassment of losing control and the terror of being truly intimate with another. Intimacy is a high risk that threatens the exposure of shame. We are distrustful and have a low tolerance of tenderness.

As children, we were expected to follow the rules without question. Obeying the rules and not causing problems were more important than having feelings and knowing the reasons for those feelings. Only people in authority had any power or could be seen and heard. Fight types create boundaries that keep what they most need at bay. It is difficult to grasp that fighting is more a plea for respect and kindness—a denied longing for our vulnerability to be seen and our significance affirmed. There are two fight types—*Dominance* and *Defiance*.

	Dominance	Defiance
Core Characteristics	Controlling Critical Judgmental Detached Independent Privileged Seeks power and status Intolerant of imperfection	Angry Blaming Hostile Defensive Cynical Self-absorbed Seeks justice and reparation Intolerant of rules/ prohibitions
When Triggered, Acts	Rejecting Withholding Superior Demanding Unforgiving Cruel Ruthless Needs to be right	Difficult Belligerent Entitled Confrontational Vindictive Hateful Revengeful
Fears	Insignificance	Unimportance
Ashamed of	Needing tenderness	Needing validation

Defense Postures	Distance from others
	Becomes critical to deny
	  the need for intimacy
		Blames others
		Becomes belligerent to deny
		  the need for intimacy

As a child	Felt overcontrolled or
	  ignored
	Had to learn things the
	  hard way on her own
	Expected to behave as
	  an adult
		Felt overcontrolled or
		  overindulged
		Given too much freedom or
		  not enough
		Expected to do as she was
		  told, or else

Emotional Challenges	Trust Significance	Trust Respect
Shadow Rage Disguise	Dependence	Devotion
Wisdom	Discernment	Truth-telling

DOMINANCE DISGUISE OF RAGE

We know we wear the *Dominance* disguise of rage when we have a life pattern of control. Sometimes we control others, but mostly we will do everything we can not to be controlled. Controlling is our way of keeping shame under wraps. We consider ourselves top dog—a self-appointed judge, which gives us the privilege to evaluate the character of others while we determine our level of emotional investment. Operating from the arrogance of our mental courthouse, we judge what is right and wrong. We have tendencies toward greed and power. Our views are as razor-sharp as they are narrow. We bring unreachable standards to our relationships and hold others accountable to them.

We are deliberate, efficient, and skillful in getting what we want. While we are capable of making good decisions, our self-interest is often at the expense of others, and our critical nature causes others to feel inept and worthless in the process. We prefer positions where we can judge, control, and direct others—roles that keep us apart and elevated from others. We choose to be right over being liked, and prefer to be alone instead of dealing with what we consider to be the incompetence of others. We use our strength to keep people at a distance and even separated from one another. We generally avoid joining groups and have a low need for inclusion. We despise groupies, considering them copycats and chameleons. We are more a loner or creator of our own circumstances. Regardless of where we are, we are in charge, at least of ourselves. If we do not have the official role, we claim it. We believe that if we are not in control, others will make a mess that we will eventually have to clean up.

We do not have a conscious relationship with fear. We are likely to be oblivious as to how we enrage and frighten others. We appear indifferent to our contribution to problems. We deny that we have needs. We may not overtly invest in building intimate relationships because we deny we need them. We have convinced ourselves that we do not need others when we are honestly more ashamed of needing them. We deny this need because what accommodates intimacy is a loss of control, and to lose control is to feel ashamed, and to feel ashamed is to remember what must always be forgotten—early childhood traumas, where we felt powerless. We rarely if ever say "I'm sorry" because it assumes we *need* to be forgiven.

The nature of our relationships is driven by how much control we have over cloning others in our image. We have an intolerance of imperfection—anything that is not to our liking. The rage rules we insist on in most relationships are:

Dominance Rule #1: Don't challenge or disobey me!

Dominance Rule #2: Don't try to change me!

Dominance Rule #3: Don't accuse me of being incompetent, needy, or helpless!

Dominance Rule #4: Don't expect me to regard you as higher or better than me in any way!

Dominance Rule #5: Don't expect me to explain or apologize for what I do!

When anyone breaks these rage rules and takes a stand against us, we become aggravated, impatient, and determined to prove them wrong. In response, others may become frightened and attempt to reduce the tension. They may not feel they have a choice other than giving us what we want because of the influence we have or the dependency they have on us.

Generally we feel entitled to express rage toward others, but our disguise of *Dominance* hides the hurt we feel from being misunderstood and disappointed. When others resist us, we feel ineffectual—like a failure. We are puzzled and don't understand why anyone wouldn't want to be like us. Shameful feelings lurk as the conflict persists unresolved to our satisfaction. To avoid the threat of shame, we strike out, punishing the other person through physical abuse, or by physically leaving the situation, i.e., the job, the relationship, the community, the room, etc. If it is not possible to sever the relationship physically, we emotionally detach, having nothing else to do with them. We become silent, cold, controlled, and dismissing, allowing the intensity of our rage to fill the air with mysterious discomfort and fear. We feel righteously indignant, and swear never to forgive, reserving the right to use our power against them in the future.

Underneath this bravado, an older rage wound has been awakened. We are terrified of feeling insignificant, a horror that must be obliterated to escape the shame of helplessness rooted in a childhood where we were severely controlled, and had to obey the rules or else bad things happened. Bad things *did* happen, and we were hurt when we asserted ourselves. Being obedient and following the rules were more important than having feelings, and we recognized and resented that only adults had a right to be seen and heard. We dislike that we were not able to feel significant as a child. We in no way forgave our parents for not valuing or protecting us, and we vowed never to feel helpless and hurt again. As adults, we still carry that unresolved rage, making sure we have everything we need, and never depending on anyone unless it is under our terms. While we long for tenderness and a respectful affirmation of our existence, we distrust it. We would prefer to take control than to risk drowning in shameful feelings of dependency, smallness, and helplessness—there is nothing in between. We cannot forgive and forget, and will do everything we can to feel important and safe, including hurting others.

A DAY IN THE LIFE OF BETH—*DOMINANCE*

I'm at the gym by 6:30 every morning, you know. Mom taught me long ago to stay in shape! She's eighty-three now and looking better than she feels. Oh, that reminds me. I have to take her fresh flowers when I leave here. She informed me recently that it's my time to take care of her, not that I haven't been doing that for most of my life. I don't even have a life because of her. I guess it's not the time to tell her what I truly feel given she's in that rest home dying of cancer. Of course I'll take care of her. It's my duty—my cross to bear.

Sometimes I take my sixteen-year-old daughter with me to the gym, but lately she prefers to be with her friends. She told me she was interested in locating her real parents. She seemed to emphasize "real"! Hell, she has everything a child could want—great school, fine clothes, money for frivolous things, and me. She's completely ungrateful.

I had this meeting at work this morning with my Diversity Council. The employees seemed preoccupied, angry, and afraid given the impending war, and I've been concerned about productivity and my executive bonus. I wanted to get the employees' minds off war and on work, so I asked my Council to discreetly go around and encourage employees to refocus, you know, on work. How could a request so simple result in such outrage? Hell, you give them a task and they complain. What good are they?

Elizabeth had the nerve to ask me how I felt about the war and if I were willing to guarantee people's jobs if sales went down. The rest of those assholes let her go on and on, talking down to me. Elizabeth thought I should be the one out there asking folks how they felt and talking about how I felt, and telling people they had nothing to worry about. Where does she get off? She disrespected my position as a vice president of the company paying her salary!

My only response to Elizabeth and the other spineless members of the Council that allowed her insubordination was that this was obviously a task too difficult for the Diversity Council. I then excused myself from the meeting. Elizabeth was still shouting at me as I left the room. I was irritated but not angry. I couldn't understand why she was so upset, and assumed the silence of the others meant she was their voice. I kept my cool but I was disappointed in all of them. I kind of felt sorry for them, actually. I went to my office and spent the rest of the afternoon drafting a letter to all employees informing them that if productivity did not return to a level matching last year's projections, drastic measures would be taken, including layoffs. I'm sure that this approach will get people focused on work, not war.

I picked up my daughter from school and she didn't speak to me all the way home. Once at home, she stormed off to her room slamming her door. I marched right behind her demanding that she tell me what was wrong. Before I knew anything I had slapped her and was telling her how selfish and disrespectful she was. She burst into tears and I didn't know what to do, I just knew I felt manipulated, so I left.

When I told my husband that I felt our daughter was moving away from me, he had little to say. He seemed careful not to say anything that would upset me, but everything he says upsets me. He asked me if I'd asked her what she was feeling. How ridiculous! Of course I'd asked her. Does he think I'm stupid? I get so little from him it's hard to see the point in taking anything of significance to him. He just wimps out. I'm not upset with my daughter, just confused. What is her problem? She's got everything she needs. Why is she being such an ungrateful brat? And why should I keep trying to make her life better? Hell, what has she done for me lately?

How do I feel? Kinda numb, empty, and alone.

JOURNALING QUESTIONS

1. What thoughts, feelings, memories, or sensations did you experience while reading about *Dominance*?
2. What aspect of this disguise is alive in your life?
3. Who or what does this disguise remind you of?
4. What does *Dominance* teach you about rage and the need to heal?

THE WISDOM OF DOMINANCE—DISCERNMENT

When our disguise is not ruling our world, we open more to our wisdom. The wisdom in the *Dominance* disguise of rage is discernment, discriminating awareness. Our instincts have afforded us good judgment, courage, autonomy, and clear vision. We are comfortable with our power and use it to transform our worlds. We have an inherent sense of fairness and can recognize whether a social structure is sound or weak. We will not be oppressed nor will we oppress others.

We are naturally able both to see the big picture and hold true to it with understanding and compassion.

LETTING GO

We are beginning to let go of the *Dominance* disguise of rage when:

- We can acknowledge that we are hurt and afraid.
- We become less controlling and judgmental of others and ourselves.
- We become genuinely open to what we don't know and what others can teach us.

We are on track when we acknowledge that we long to know:

- How do I love without feeling like a fool?
- How do I stay connected with others and myself when I am hurt and disappointed?
- How do I allow the good and bad in others and in myself?
- How do I say "I'm sorry" or "It was my fault"?
- How do I stop contributing to rage legacies of war, greed, oppression, indifference, and self-interest?

DEFIANCE DISGUISE OF RAGE

We know we wear the *Defiance* disguise of rage when we have a life pattern of anger and battle. Sometimes we battle outwardly with another person, place, or thing. Other times we battle within our mind or against our body. Anger is our way of keeping others, including ourselves, from noticing the shame we are feeling.

We are quick-witted and charged with energy. We can often see and feel what is wrong before others can, and put a voice to it. We prefer roles where we can have freedom, protect others and ourselves, and inflict punishment where needed. We are as quick to defend those who are less fortunate as we are to abuse them. We have strong convictions and low impulse control. While we have keen instincts, our anger blocks us from knowing what we need and getting what we want. We are quick to complain but slow to solve problems. We resent clearly stating our thoughts and feelings to others, when, in our minds, *"They should already know!"* When we are not understood, we feel rejected and become agitated. And out of this frustration and embarrassment for needing others' understanding, we become even angrier than before.

We are unable to see how we distort reality and fan the fires of our rage. When triggered, we are like a rebellious child on military duty in a solo war shooting a machine gun too large to hold. We can be belligerent, impatient, and blind to other points of view—unaware of the pain we feel and the pain we cause others. Because of this blindness, we are unable to take responsibility for our actions.

In our mind, we have paid dearly for the privilege to abuse others, just as we were abused. As a justifiable warrior in a dangerous world, we are not aware of how we create battles because we are longing for a more just outcome. However, there is never a time when we feel justice is done—somebody must pay again and again for the lost battles of our past.

We believe most people with power don't deserve it; they only abuse it. They are inadequate and fall short of our expectations. If given the chance, we believe they would take advantage of us, therefore they are the enemy. The enemy must pay for violating, exploiting, deceiving, and humiliating us and others with less power, and it is our job to see that justice is done.

In the heat of our battles, we expect the enemy to surrender while we are still firing shots—to come out with her hands held high above her head, fall on her knees, and apologize for firing the first bullet and wounding us, and to do this over and over again, for this is the apology we never received as a child. The irony is that victory in our battles never occurs. While we unconsciously long for acceptance from our enemy, we don't trust it when we receive it, and in our self-righteous aggression to defend our convictions, we become the enemy we most despise.

We are terrified of tenderness. Relationships require us to remove our battle gear, yet being disarmed makes us an obvious target for abuse. Our fears are utterly appropriate given the confusion of childhood abuse, neglect, and abandonment by those we loved and relied on. We associate love with pain. Intimacy challenges us to believe that someone could genuinely care for us, yet our survival instinct has taught us otherwise. The rage rules we insist on in relationships are:

Defiance Rule #1: Don't blame, threaten, or inconvenience me!
Defiance Rule #2: Don't place demands or expectations on me!
Defiance Rule #3: Don't expect me to forgive you!
Defiance Rule #4: Don't make a mistake! You won't get away with it!
Defiance Rule #5: Don't expect me to follow the rules!

When anyone breaks these rage rules, we become suspicious, unforgiving, and intimidating. We feel justified to fight—attack, blame, criticize, and if necessary, abuse, when we are, in fact, afraid and disappointed. We overreact to disappointments without recognizing that we are hurting and hungry for connection. We pretend to be unaffected and smug while denying our pain. In our guardedness, we distrust expressions of compassion and kindness that may come our way.

We come from childhoods where we felt we were victims of a disadvantaged war, unprepared for battle. We were silenced, threatened, and abused by authority. It was then that we made an agreement with ourselves that when we grew up, we would never be violated again. As adults, we are still armed for war. We carry feelings of being humiliated, disrespected, and devalued. *Defiance* has become a way of hiding our shame of needing to be loved. It diverts us from the rage we feel toward our own helplessness, and the longing to be honored and respected. Yet, we are unable to discern that not everyone is the enemy. We are the last one to know that some wars have ended, and that there are new ways to survive that allow us to remove our armor, rest in our own skin, and heal.

A DAY IN THE LIFE OF ANTOINETTE—*DEFIANCE*

I was late so I didn't have time to pick up my double espresso at my favorite coffeehouse. The damn bridge was backed up again, so I did what made sense to me under the circumstances—I drove in the car pool lane.

I was driving along, feeling like a free woman, singing "Respect" with Aretha on the radio. And would you believe I got pulled over by the police! I kept my cool and said nothing, but in my head, I was saying, "This asshole!"

I was pissed off that the officer asked me to turn my radio down so he could take his time telling me how wrong I was. He goes to his car to write me a ticket and it takes forever! He seemed to be enjoying wasting my time, as if I had nothing else to do. Hell, why did he think I was speeding in the first damn place?

When he finally decided to "free me from jail" I drove away screaming in my car and beating the steering wheel. I started screaming at the rubberneckers who were staring at me, turning the bridge into a stadium parking lot. Damn, women are always targets. The police would have never acted that way toward a man, I'm sure of it. I'm going to fight this ticket. It's pure discrimination.

Of all the days, the meeting started on time—thirty-five minutes ago. Everyone stopped and looked at me, just like the rubberneckers on the bridge. I wanted to scream, "What am I? Flypaper for freaks?" Instead, I took my seat without saying a word. My manager rolls her eyes my way, as if to say, "This is the third time this month you've been late." I say to myself, "Hell, I know how to count!" I'm in no mood to be messed with.

The meeting was a bore, as usual. It's amazing we get anything done. I looked at Ralph and visualized putting duct tape over his mouth. Then there was Frances talking on and on. I wanted to say, "I can see your point, but I still think you're full of shit." I couldn't seem to erase the sarcastic grin on my face and noticed that I was slowly turning my head as if to say, "What a circus!"

As my manager closed the meeting, I wondered, "Who in hell appointed her queen?" I silently found a million things wrong with her. I added this million to yesterday's list. It took all of my control not to say, "Thank you. We're all inspired by your worthless point of view." Instead, I sat silent with a hostile smirk that kept others at bay—they knew not to ask so I didn't have to tell. I left the meeting feeling like my time had been wasted. I thought, "Damn, and I got a ticket for this? These are a bunch of idiots."

My secretary stopped me in the hall. She wanted to talk about how I'd been treating her. Abrasive was her word. Why in hell is she so wimpy? She has such low self-esteem. Men don't have to apologize for being bastards, but women always have to apologize for being bitches. What's the difference, they both start with "b"! I didn't have time for her nonsense so I told her, "Get over it!"

Later, I completed several work deadlines while drinking a bottle of wine. My partner finally came home. What I really wanted was for her to notice that I had a difficult day and hold me, to tell me everything would be okay tomorrow—let's love today away. But looking at her not looking at me, I was convinced that wouldn't happen. Hell, who needs her anyway? Before I knew it I was screaming at her "You're late! Where have you been?" She quietly turned around and left the house again. I went to bed angry, hurt, and misunderstood. I tossed all night and pretended like I was asleep when she came home at 4:00 A.M. I don't know when I went to sleep. I woke up feeling like I had had a horrible dream only to realize it was my life and had been for many years.

JOURNALING QUESTIONS

1. What thoughts, feelings, memories, or sensations did you experience while reading about *Defiance*?
2. What aspect of this disguise is alive in your life?
3. Who or what does this disguise remind you of?
4. What does *Defiance* teach you about rage and the need to heal?

THE WISDOM OF DEFIANCE—TRUTH-TELLING

When *Defiance* is not ruled by a pressing anxiety for justice, its bright, warrior spirits can show up with more heart. When there is injustice in our environment, we are the first to feel it. When we, or others, are suppressed or constrained, our spirit rebels. As our rage child heals, these deep instincts can be an even greater gift. Truth-telling, courage, freedom of expression, and choice flowing from a compassionate heart—these are the necessities of our spirit. Our keen sense of justice can give us a life of independence and self-respect, and be a gift that unites the world.

LETTING GO

We are beginning to let go of the *Defiance* disguise of rage when:

- We become less armored—vindictive, angry, and accusatory—and more considerate of how we negatively and positively affect others.
- We can embrace the human frailties of others and ourselves.
- We can experience our truth instead of defending it.

We are on track when we acknowledge that we long to know:

- How can I love and be loved without hurting others and myself?
- What would happen if I didn't have to prove I was right?
- How do I fight for justice and not suffer?
- How do I say "I'm sorry" and mean it?
- How do I stop contributing to rage legacies of violence, hatred, abuse, and disrespect?

5

Flight Types—
On the Run from Rage!

Distraction and *Devotion*—at a Glance

Those of us who are Flight types find ways to escape the intense and painful truth we embody. We don't rock the boat. We are more likely to give in to avoid conflict. We feel *I must pay,* then we harbor silent resentment. We may live beyond our means, spending recklessly or borrowing money, even giving money away. We reveal little of our true selves to others. Instead, we become generous to distract others when we are feeling unworthy and inadequate. We tend to have poor emotional boundaries, and can be targets of use and abuse. We are guilt-driven and impulsive, and occasionally have surprising outbursts of rage that shame us back into being overly nice. Flight types exert tremendous effort outside of themselves. We are image conscious, wanting to be seen as good servants. We over-function to avoid *feeling* in general, and feeling alone, exiled, or abandoned in particular. It is difficult to grasp that pretending and serving are more accurately petitions for acceptance and ways to guarantee that we will always be seen, special, and needed. There are two Flight types—*Distraction* and *Devotion*.

	Distraction	Devotion
Core Characteristics	Incessant	Accommodates
	Urgent	Avoids
	Compulsive	Over-functions
	Consumptive	Guilt-ridden
	Envious	Resentful
	Hedonistic	Denies the truth
	Seeks immediate pleasure by overindulging	Seeks significance by pleasing
	Intolerant of stillness	Intolerant of separation
When Triggered, Acts	Pretender, denies problems	Martyr, guilt-inducing
	Self-indulgent	Self-sacrificing
	Performs	Pleases
	Jealous rages	Hurt rages
	Needs to be seen	Needs to be needed
Fears	Inadequacy	Unworthiness
Ashamed of	Needing nourishment	Needing admiration
Defense Posture	Overindulges in tasks or material acquisitions	Clings by accommodating others
	Self-defeating to avoid intimacy	Self-sacrificing to avoid intimacy
As a child	Frightened and anxious	Doubtful, voiceless, guilty
	Felt trapped and confused	Felt unworthy of love
	Performed for praise	Pleased for praise
	Expected to be better than others	Expected to put others first
Emotional Challenges	Intimacy	Self-respect
	Stillness	Independence
Shadow Rage Disguise	Depression	Defiance
Wisdom	Free will	Harmony

DISTRACTION DISGUISE OF RAGE

We know we wear *Distraction* as our disguise of rage when we have a life pattern of searching, seeking, reaching, and achieving for more. Most of our energy is invested in the external world. We are intellectual and charismatic and we know how to make others feel good. We generally play leading roles in life. We prefer independent and solo acts where our starring role is clear. Politics, technology, sales, and public speaking are well suited for our disguise. We have great vision and can be bored with here-and-now reality. We are more in touch with our intellect than our emotions. Therefore, we can come across as smart, sarcastic, humorous, and unkind in one brief interaction.

We can be intensity junkies, sensation seekers, and adventurers, and can get as lost in a single task as we do in multiple tasks. Many associate us with having various addictions or having an addictive personality. While this may be true, all of us, regardless of our disguises, may struggle with addictions, not just those of us who wear *Distraction*. We will typically have several activities we partake in for immediate gratification—eating, shopping, spending, achieving, working, relating, drugging, drinking—anything we enjoy or do well is likely to be done in excess and become a *Distraction*. We are generally good at what we do but not always present in what we are doing. Because we multitask and are obsessive, we tend to overextend ourselves, run behind schedule, and make commitments we cannot keep. Then we resent others when they express disappointment.

Silently, we feel we are worth waiting for. We will arrive to important appointments on time for curtain call, even if we are up all night obsessively working to make things perfect. But more commonly, appointments are changed, travel is rearranged, details are lost—constant chaos is all a part of the fast life. We rush from one appointment to the next seemingly without breathing. We even rush to our meditation practice! We tend to be more concerned with how we perform or appear to others than how we feel within ourselves.

The idea is to speed through life and to maintain this speed as long as we can without limits and often despite consequences. We tend to ignore the sensations of our body and prefer an altered state that allows us to live high above the lows of life. Therefore, our body takes a beating. We are likely to find ourselves shocked and incapacitated with accidents or illnesses because we move too fast to notice early-warning signs.

We are restless, emotionally ravenous, and often excessive. We resist being idle, unaware that we are afraid that in our stillness our memories will devour us. So we keep busy stuffing ourselves with material gains and activities from the outside world hoping it will quiet the inner terror of inadequacy, emptiness, and loneliness. We must be adored; not because we feel adorable, but because we feel empty if we have no proof of our value—a proof we must be able to point to outside of ourselves.

While we bring spontaneous joy to our relationships and entertain those around us with our various talents, few people really know us intimately. We are afraid that if people got too close we would disappoint them and be uncovered as a fraud. While we prefer to be seen as charming, intelligent, professional, and sociable, in conflict we can swing in the opposite direction and become explosive, aloof, or sarcastic. When this happens, the adoration we have grown to rely on from others is threatened. Therefore, the rage rules we insist on in relationships are:

Distraction Rule #1: Don't expect me to sit still and relax!

Distraction Rule #2: Don't expect me to be emotionally vulnerable!

Distraction Rule #3: Don't tell me I'm not perfect!

Distraction Rule #4: Don't expect me to waste time being upset or depressed!

Distraction Rule #5: Don't expect me to have enough of anything!

The *Distraction* disguise takes exception to anything or anyone that attempts to bring us down. We like to keep things informative, not personal. Emotionally we like to tread water with our hopes and dreams rather than deep-sea dive with the truth. We seek knowledge that offers immediate comfort, not necessarily wisdom. For example, we are more likely to write a check toward a problem to avoid any emotional experience of it, or we make a quick decision or comply with a decision to avoid conflict. We have a low tolerance for conflict or discomfort. We want to do something—anything—to relieve the situation and move on.

In relationships, we want to feel good. Typically, we are not aware of problems unless someone else points them out. When this occurs, we are shocked and ashamed of the truth it reveals. We feel flawed, blamed, and criticized. This exposure must be hidden, so we become belligerent to distance ourselves from the shame. Often, we explode in rage, taking this opportunity to complain about the inequities in the relationship, something, up until now, we had ignored or denied. We don't want any problems, period! We want to fast-forward through pain and discomfort and consume the desserts of life in one sensational gorge. Once the conflict has settled, we want to move back into our comfort lane and proceed with life as usual—all is forgotten until the next time someone brings it up.

Those of us wearing the *Distraction* disguise have shameful memories of feeling blamed, criticized, and humiliated for disappointing someone we depended on as children. We felt punished or ignored for not trying hard *enough* and not being good *enough*. Our life depended on how we performed, and often, how we performed was more important than who we were. Wearing the lifelong pattern of *Distraction* means we do everything we can to ignore feelings of emptiness and inadequacy. We are emotionally and often physically rushing through our lives to escape intolerable shame. We obsessively feed our insatiable emotional appetite with fast food while denying the haunting truth of our hunger.

A DAY IN THE LIFE OF CARMEN—*DISTRACTION*

Lately, life has been a whirlwind. My father has been in the hospital for the past four weeks, I've changed jobs twice, and of course, the obvious, I weigh quite a bit more than before. But you know, I just have to roll with it. Besides, I consider myself fabulously full!

My new job is great. I'm the first woman to serve in my position and the only woman on the management team. Everyone expects me to succeed, so I do, but a lot is required. I attend one meeting after another, often in different states. I can usually get by, you know, pull it off without any major glitches. Hell, the meetings only last an hour and then I'm off to the next thing. Sometimes other people want to sweat the small stuff, but I just ignore them. It's no big deal. Well, it shouldn't be. Actually I was doing quite well with all this until yesterday.

In the middle of an important meeting, a horrendous sadness flooded me for no reason and tears began streaming down my face uncontrollably. Everybody froze and looked at me. I politely left the room and it took me several minutes to regroup. I was so happy no one ran behind me to see what had happened. I couldn't have explained it. I was more angry because of the inconvenience, and I worried about what others thought about my quick exit. I was also frightened over this surprise attack of emotions and didn't know how to make sure it would never happen again. I can't remember the last time I cried. Maybe thirty years ago. It's just not me!

On the way home, I stopped by my favorite takeout and ordered enough food for an army. I don't know what got into me but I had to have everything I wanted. When I got home, I felt tangled in my thoughts. I worried about what I did, didn't do, should have done, and shouldn't have done. It was starting to freak me out. I ate and had a few beers, but I was more anxious than usual. My father called from the hospital down in the dumps about his situation. I had to stop what I was doing and put on a happy face to comfort him, but I wasn't in the mood for it, really. When I hung up the phone I felt pure rage and resentment. He's a grown man and expects me to mother him. It makes me want to scream!

I called some of my friends. We usually party together on the weekends. We may overindulge in food, light drugs, and alcohol, but it's not a daily endeavor, more a way to let loose, relax, and give our minds a break. We can afford our habits and we mind our own business. They came right over and we were up most of the night. When I'm with my friends, it's usually my job to entertain them. Sometimes it feels more like work but I seem to make energy for it somehow. Besides it's fun and it beats being alone, especially last night.

But of all the nights, my friend Silvia had to ask me point-blank what was wrong. Why in hell did she do that? I felt she had crawled underneath my skin and was deliberately trying to bring me down. I don't remember how I replied. I didn't have time for that nonsense. Besides, more and more, these friends seem superficial and boring, and I'm feeling less satisfied around them.

I guess I'm a little stressed but I have nothing to complain about, really. I'm healthy, educated, well traveled, and make good money. Hell, I'm a success story! So why, then, do I feel so empty when I'm so full?

JOURNALING QUESTIONS

1. What thoughts, feelings, memories, or sensations did you experience while reading about *Distraction*?
2. What aspect of this disguise is alive in your life?
3. Who or what does this disguise remind you of?
4. What does *Distraction* teach you about rage and the need to heal?

THE WISDOM OF DISTRACTION—FREE WILL

When we begin to slow down, to soften and rest in our yearning, the wisdom of our spirit begins to emerge. We become more balanced, and find that we have been "looking for love in all the wrong places" and return home, to our bodies, to love ourselves first. Our spirit is a natural antenna for freedom, beauty, generosity, spontaneous joy, and inspiration. When we begin to rest in our own fullness, this goodness can find expression in our relationships, our creative work, and in our environment.

LETTING GO

We are beginning to let go of the *Distraction* disguise of rage when:

- We begin to do less and feel more.
- We are less self-indulgent and consumptive and more thoughtful and appreciative of what we have.
- We invest in the well-being of our body.

We are on track when we acknowledge that we long to know:

- How do I do nothing without being consumed by fear?
- Who am I without "things"?
- What happens to me if I stop running?
- What do I have to give back to the world?
- How do I stop contributing to rage legacies of greed, indifference, waste, and class oppression?

DEVOTION DISGUISE OF RAGE

We know we wear the *Devotion* disguise of rage when we have a life pattern of pleasing. Pleasing is our way of dealing with the terror we feel when others are unhappy or express negative emotions. We are protective of those we love and feel responsible for their emotional comforts and discomforts. It's as if whatever others feel is our fault—if it's good, that's our doing. If it's bad, that's our fault and more disturbing.

We pride ourselves on knowing how to help. We enjoy negotiating, interceding, and peacekeeping. We have convinced ourselves that we have a sixth sense about what others need and we are the right person to give it to them. We like to be seen as nice, good, kind, and generous. Maintaining this image is safer than exposing the terror and resentment we feel but don't understand and therefore deny.

We are intuitive, caring, responsible, and strong-minded. People rely on us to bring heart to a situation and be there for them. We are associated with being a caretaker and perfectionist, and we bring a repertoire of comforting interventions to our relationships. While we are capable and in control, our need to make what we consider to be bad emotions better stifles the growth of others. It is difficult for us to understand how being devoted to others is a detour from taking care of or knowing ourselves.

We are convinced that we must first make sure others feel good before we can enjoy our life. This, of course, is an impossible task. Yet we feel guilty and unworthy if we live happily out loud while others are unhappy, especially those we love. This fact is not only enraging but also demanding because we feel we must drop what we are doing to accommodate others. While our devotion to others is genuine, it has a dual motivation. We want to see others feel good because we care about them *and* because their not feeling good has an alarming impact on us. We tend to expend tremendous energy on people and things we don't have control over while limiting the potential of our life experiences.

Those of us who wear the mask of *Devotion* are social beings and invest heavily in relationships. We enjoy the company of others, especially if we can accommodate them in some small or large way. Regardless of where we are, we appear to be gladly helping others, but the nature of our relationships is driven by how much safety we can guarantee. We believe that if we are not keeping things comfortable, others will become upset. Therefore, the rage rules we insist on in most relationships are:

Devotion Rule #1: Don't expect me to stop worrying about you!
Devotion Rule #2: Don't be unhappy!
Devotion Rule #3: Don't push me away or close me out!
Devotion Rule #4: Don't make me feel unneeded!
Devotion Rule #5: Don't expect me to stop trying to help!

When anyone breaks these rage rules, we become terrified that life will get out of control, other people will become upset, and we will be harshly blamed for it. *Devotion* feeds the faulty assumption we carry that if we care for others, we will always be needed and never blamed, criticized, or disappointed. We deny that our generosity toward the emotional needs of others is our way of purchasing their undying gratitude. The problem with this deal is that it is often without the other person's awareness or agreement.

We have poor boundaries. The problems of others become our priorities. We overextend and overcommit because we must please. We typically say *yes* when we want to say *no*, then rationalize the goodness of our *yes* and deny the truth of our *no*. Our habit of self-sacrificing serves its purpose as long as the perception of *good* and *nice* is maintained. The only time there are problems is when others bring them up.

We often suffer physically because our bodies absorb the pain we deny, contributing to us being targets for inner hardening (fibroids, kidney stones, cancer, etc.) and immune deficiencies. We hide our pain, shame, and resentment to deny our own rage and to avoid being a target of rage. We make this sacrifice, both willingly and unwillingly, and therefore, we don't understand why others don't do the same.

When others complain, we feel guilty and responsible, and are quick to apologize. Silently we feel we don't deserve what is happening, but we are unable to defend ourselves. We detest having to feel anything but good. To avert the pain we grin and bear it, and do whatever is necessary to make peace in the moment, at any cost.

We can be sarcastic, and in rare moments we may break down

and explode in a rage of tears, spewing the buried resentments we've long denied while singing the tune of: *After all I've done for you, how could you! Shame on you!* People are shocked to hear the bitterness dripping from our once-soothing lips. Others feel deceived and betrayed by the absence of the happy face that we've worn and they have come to rely on. They say *I didn't know you felt that way*, while we think to ourselves *I didn't know I felt this way either*. But these cruel surprise acts are disguises to mask our shame of failing to please. While our explosions punish our offenders, we feel guilty for hurting them. To compensate, we once again begin to overextend ourselves, and the vicious cycle continues.

Underneath this perceived kindness and service to others lies a burning rage wound. We are terrified of feeling negative emotions and of being a target of them, a horror that must be obliterated to escape the shame and helplessness rooted in a childhood where we felt blamed, criticized, or humiliated for disappointing someone we desperately relied on. As a child, we felt this injustice was our fault. Despite our best efforts, we felt like a failure and vowed to work harder and never to be humiliated again. As a frightened child in an adult body, we are still searching for forgiveness. We believe that if we demonstrate our undying love *enough*, we will be pardoned. We desperately need to please others while denying our desperate need to be pleased. Inside we feel like a *bad* girl, unworthy of being loved. Beneath this shame lives the *enraged* girl, the one we are terrified to bring to light.

A DAY IN THE LIFE OF THERESA—*DEVOTION*

Sometimes I feel like the little old lady who lives in a shoe. Had so many children she didn't know what to do. By this age, I thought my kids would be taking care of me. But it isn't working out that way. My daughter, Tia, and her two kids have been living with me for the past six months. I'm so happy that she has finally left her husband, who was so abusive to her. I worked so hard to help her to see that she needed to leave him. This was her second abusive relationship. I worry sometimes that my relationship with her father affected her ability to make healthy choices. So I'm trying even harder to help out now.

My grandkids are in shock. They are acting out a lot. I know it's hard for them and they are angry. I try to be supportive and show them how much I care, but they don't seem to want to let me get close. The only time they stop fighting is when the TV is on, which nowadays is night and day. I end up hiding out in my room just to get away from the noise of it.

I'm still in shock about last year, when I was away on a work assignment overseas and I let my daughter and my son Ralph stay at the house. I had just refinanced the house to post bail for Ralph. He got into a bit of trouble with the law but he's a good kid. He needed a place to stay, and there was plenty of room, since I was going to be away. We talked about it, and he and Tia agreed to pay the house note. Well, they never did. The house was foreclosed! I was furious at the time. But they swear I didn't explain about the mortgage payments to them. I'm sure I did, but maybe I wasn't clear enough. I guess I should have known that they had too much on their minds to carry that responsibility. Now the house is gone. It's such a blow. I'm struggling to see any silver lining. We're all crammed in this small apartment. I try to tell myself that material things aren't what's most important; it's loving relationships that matter.

One good thing is that Tia is finally getting a divorce. The legal part of it is complicated, and I've been trying to help. When I went to court with her she really froze up in front of the lawyer and judge, so I told them everything she was having trouble saying. When we got home, she started slamming doors and wouldn't talk to me for days. I had to do everything—cook, clean, take care of the kids, and she never offered to help. And then she got in my face screaming about how she was grown and didn't need me to defend her. That really felt like a slap in the face, after all I had done. I really lost my temper, too. But later I felt guilty, and I realized it must be hard on her pride to realize she made such a mess of things. I know the divorce is upsetting, but she really shouldn't take it out on me.

Now Ralph is back in jail. It's the alcohol that keeps getting him in trouble. Tia drinks, too. I'm trying to convince them to cut back. Sometimes, my advice seems to be helping. Other times, not. Their father was an alcoholic. Maybe it's genetic. I can understand the temptation to drink, but I can't let myself do it. There are too many people depending on me.

How can I be surrounded by so much heartache? Seems like nearly everyone I know is in some kind of crisis. Sometimes it feels like such a burden on me. I can hardly take it, but I can't stop. My friends say I shouldn't get so involved, but how do you just let people suffer when you love them?

JOURNALING QUESTIONS

1. What thoughts, feelings, memories, or sensations did you experience while reading about *Devotion*?
2. What aspect of this disguise is alive in your life?
3. Who or what does this disguise remind you of?
4. What does *Devotion* teach you about rage and the need to heal?

THE WISDOM OF DEVOTION—HARMONY

When the fear and emptiness that has driven us begins to ease, our gifts fully emerge—compassion, empathy, intimacy, and belonging woven with kind attention toward our own needs. Deep, loving relationships, with others and ourselves, are the necessity of our spirit. We are highly attuned to the subtle energies around us, both physical and emotional. We have the instincts of a healer—naturally patient, tenderhearted, accepting, and forgiving. Our commitment to harmony makes us one who weaves the fabric of community into a force for good—a quality that naturally overflows from a well-nurtured spirit that maintains levelheadedness and level-heartedness.

LETTING GO

We are beginning to let go of the *Devotion* disguise of rage when:

- We begin to set healthy boundaries for ourselves and maintain them.
- We stop betraying ourselves by pretending to please.
- We start hearing and responding to our own cries.

We are on track when we acknowledge that we long to know:

- How do I love without giving myself away?
- How do I not take responsibility for how others feel?
- How do I take care of myself without feeling selfish?
- How do I allow others to care for me?
- How do I stop contributing to rage legacies of martyrdom, denial, and abusing the feminine?

6

Shrink Types—
Hide and Seek from Rage

Dependence and *Depression*—at a Glance

Shrink types feel overwhelmed with life. We accommodate to avoid conflict then convince ourselves that we don't have a choice. We feel too small emotionally to fight, so we are likely to give up and sabotage ourselves, and then feel ashamed. We can be silent and passive, and live in the shadows of others, supporting them and living vicariously through them. We expect those we support to notice us, represent us, speak for us, and take care of us. We are afraid that if we show our full selves in the world, we will hurt or disappoint others, or we will be harmed. At the same time, we are silently enraged over living small and as imposters. We hide our resentment and, while we try to hide guilt, we are less successful. Our agreement with life is to *shrink*—not exist too loudly or largely. Because we chose to survive, we must manipulate the world around us to intervene on our behalf. It is difficult to grasp that shrinking is more accurately a game of hide and seek, where the job of life is for others to find us and reassure us that life is worth living.

	Dependence	Depression
Core Characteristics	Sweet Childlike Gullible Seductive Cautious Manipulates to be rescued Intolerant of adult responsibility	Bitter Disheartened Indifferent Avoids Withdrawn Manipulates to be seen Intolerant of adult expectations
When Triggered, Acts	Fearful Confused Mute Helpless Insecure Inhibited Needs to be helped Easily influenced	Withholding Indifferent Inaccessible Mopes Hopeless Reserved Needs to be alone Becomes invisible
Fears	Abandonment	Engagement
Ashamed of	Needing to be cherished	Needing to be seen
Defense Postures	Hides own talents to be taken care of Hopes to be rescued Becomes helpless to avoid the shame of being a woman	Hides own talents to avoid intimacy Hopes to be discovered Becomes hopeless to avoid the shame of being seen
As a child	Felt deprived and abandoned Unable to do things on one's own Seen but not heard Had to stay childlike to guarantee love	Felt deprived and deserted Unable to openly grieve losses Unseen and unheard Had to stay invisible to guarantee safety
Emotional Challenges	Independence Separation	Existence Intimacy
Shadow Rage Disguise	Dominance	Distraction
Wisdom	Originality	Solitude

DEPENDENCE DISGUISE OF RAGE

We know we wear the *Dependence* disguise of rage when we have a life pattern of uncertainty. Being uncertain is our way of being certain that someone is always there, for if this were not so, we would feel lost, afraid, and ashamed. We commonly move through life dependent on the support of others, like a child who *could* take its first step but is afraid that once she does, she will never be held again. We prefer the safety of being held to the risk of walking and *maybe* falling. Fundamentally, we are ashamed of standing on our own, so we play life safe and avoid risks that affirm our adulthood.

We *play* at being grown-up—dreaming about how we want to be some day while denying that we *are* grown-up, or dreaming about a better tomorrow when tomorrow was yesterday. We believe that life should be easy, not hard, and that the universe *will* provide. We expect to be cared for and we feel we deserve freedom without effort or responsibility. We are young at heart, thoughtful, and imaginative, and prefer roles where we can be helpful, original, and needed.

Generally, life feels unfair. We feel overburdened and under-supported. We resent the expectations that come with being an adult—earning money, making decisions, being agreeable, being a wife, being a mother, making others happy, knowing what you want, and taking care of yourself. We want to have fun, live in this moment without worrying about the next, but we often find ourselves in emotional and financial distress. While we are capable of generating creative ideas that support our well-being, we seldom feel confident accomplishing them. It is not that we are afraid of succeeding; we are more afraid of losing the affiliation of others if we become self-reliant, so we therefore promote an *appearance* of helplessness. Being helpless is our way to guarantee connection. Unfortunately, it is at the expense of our emotional growth.

We find it difficult to assert ourselves because it might upset someone we rely on and jeopardize their needed support. We don't feel entitled, i.e., *old enough, smart enough, experienced enough, grown-up enough*, to have such power. Instead of risking the disapproval or loss of others we depend on, we smile, voiceless, in insincere compliance, taking the path of least resistance. We make decisions to appease others, believing we must kiss up to them to avoid being left on our own. We feel stuck between needing others to protect us and not knowing what to do for ourselves if they don't. But underneath this disguise of helpless deceit is pure rage and intolerable shame because we feel we must sacrifice freedom in exchange for affiliation. We commonly feel betrayed and disappointed, and terrified of our thoughts. We may become ill or our lives completely explode around us, forcing others to notice and hopefully come to our rescue.

Long ago, survival meant that *children should be seen but not heard*. While we know as adults that this is not true, we still feel paralyzed in this old role we were forced to assume. We perceive our value as located outside of ourselves. We tend to attach ourselves to powerful people, places, and things and serve them with unquestioned and often blind loyalty. These include parents, teachers, religions, schools, children, friends, work, and the like. None of these affiliations are necessarily a problem, but when we use them to hide and avoid the responsibilities of living, we perpetuate our dependence and stunt our growth. In this regard, our loyalty is more a desperate plea to be valued than a true expression of our thinking.

We have convinced ourselves that it is impossible to accomplish what we want without support from others; therefore, most of our relationships are based on how others can help us feel better about ourselves. The rage rules we insist on in most relationships are:

Dependence Rule #1: Don't expect me to know or do what's best for me!

Dependence Rule #2: Don't expect me to get angry, confront conflict, or take a risk!

Dependence Rule #3: Don't expect me to be more confident than those I admire!

Dependence Rule #4: Don't expect me to grow up and stop needing you!

Dependence Rule #5: Don't ignore me or stop taking care of me!

When anyone breaks these rage rules, we are offended and often
may even cry about it. On the inside we feel enraged, terrified, and
helpless. Our biggest concern is being abandoned, so we feel we must
do what we can to make nice and maintain our status of belonging,
which often means keeping silent, *like a good girl*. This compromise
only further contributes to our feelings of shame, which in turn leads
to more rage.

Our relationships tend to be polite but lack intimacy. We are envious of others who appear to have their lives together. We feel small in
comparison to them. What others have is always better than what we
have—they are bigger and better. We are unaware that we seek surro-
gate parenting in most of our relationships. In our mind, it is someone else's job to affirm us. When frustrated, *They should know what I
need!* is a common mind-set. We expect those with power to notice
us and take care of us. We allow others to control us, blindly trusting
that they will spare us the dread of growing wiser. We rationalize our
faith in others, but inevitably, they disappoint us and we feel betrayed
and abandoned.

It feels *right* that others are greater than we are. As a child, we had
to maintain our child status to be loved. We were rewarded for being
a good *little* girl and felt we were punished for being independent. We
lived in intense fear of expressing ourselves, overdoing something,
not knowing how to behave or whom to please. We resented that we
were not affirmed or encouraged to be self-sufficient, and we are still
seeking this affirmation. Yet, to affirm ourselves as capable adults is
to compete with authority, i.e., our parents, managers, etc., and we
don't trust that we can succeed without losing something or someone
of grave emotional or financial importance.

A DAY IN THE LIFE OF PATRICIA—*DEPENDENCE*

I'm doing the best I can but dammmmmmn! I feel buried alive! The minute I get one problem solved, another one appears. I guess money is my biggest problem. I'm in a lot of debt, but I can usually make a deal with the creditors if I remember to call. My check was garnished recently for back taxes, and they didn't even warn me. I asked the IRS for a break, but they told me "No!" Being nice didn't seem to have any effect on them. Thank goodness my parents helped me out.

My job is overwhelming! I know that they appreciate my loyalty but they don't tell me enough how much they value what I do. Actually, I stopped liking my job years ago when they promoted me into management. It was a major decision—one I didn't really make but went along with because we ran out of time. I didn't know whether to take the position and make them happy or stay where I was and make myself happy. I chose to take the position, and now I wonder if either of us is happy. I don't know.

Recently, my handsome tax advisor suggested I purchase a house. I said yes before I really thought about it. I wanted him to be impressed with my independence and maybe ask me out on a date. That didn't happen. Meanwhile, I had purchased this damn house! My parents helped me out, even packed me up and moved me in, but I'm not sure I even wanted this house, especially on my own. Hell, I thought I'd be married by now with two kids and a white picket fence. Instead, I'm forty, single, depend on my parents financially, and need this job that I don't like so I can pay for this house that I don't want.

It's been a nightmare from day one. The movers promised three times to deliver my furniture from storage but they never showed up. Each time I had to take off work and wait all day. I couldn't pin them down with a time. Well, I didn't try. They were demanding on the phone and I didn't want to fight with them. I just rearranged my schedule but then they never showed. When they finally came, several of my cherished pieces were missing and two items were broken. They didn't offer any compensation. I didn't push for it either. I just wanted them to go away. They finally found my missing furniture. They called me on a Wednesday to deliver on Thursday. Again, I had to change my plans even though it was my birthday. I was afraid to say no. Besides, I wanted it to all be over. My best friend got angry and told me I should have set a time and demanded compensation. He told me I was being a doormat. I felt hurt, like I had been dishonest with myself. I became ill and felt down, and was in bed for the next few days.

I make enough money but creditors always seem to take it before I see it, and I never seem to have enough. I like to shop and eat, but who doesn't? I had a roommate but she moved out after four months. She wasn't very sociable. I'm not sure what I'll do next. I get tired thinking about it. I could sell the house. Maybe I could reduce my monthly payments if I refinanced. Dad did all this paperwork when I bought the house. Maybe he'd be willing to do it again. My Dad! He's the best!

Maybe I need to get away and have some fun. No, too many deadlines at work and I've taken a number of sick days already this year. My food consultant is concerned about my blood pressure and wants me to relax, cook organic meals, and meditate before bed. I'm not doing any of it, really. I start cooking about 8:00 P.M. after checking my e-mails. The rest of the night I watch TV or read the newspaper. Sometimes I'll eat sweets, especially now that I don't have a roommate. By the time I go to bed it's 11:30 P.M. and I'm up at 5:30 A.M. Mom usually calls early in the morning. She says it's the only time she can catch me, but I know it's to wake me up and help me on my way. Mom's the word! My only problem is that I have too many bills to have fun.

JOURNALING QUESTIONS

1. What thoughts, feelings, memories, or sensations did you experience while reading about *Dependence*?

2. What aspect of this disguise is alive in your life?
3. Who or what does this disguise remind you of?
4. What does *Dependence* teach you about rage and the need to heal?

THE WISDOM OF DEPENDENCE—ORIGINALITY

When the veils of fear are lifted, our natural gift of originality shines true. We are cheerful, trusting, and discover with ease the wonders of life. Our spirit enjoys celebration and creativity. We open wide to joy and can laugh at our mistakes. We naturally delight in the oneness of all beings. Playfulness, insight, magic, and inspiration are our gifts and our offerings to the world.

LETTING GO

We are beginning to let go of the *Dependence* disguise of rage when:

- We shift from being confused, doubtful, and helpless to taking control of the details of our lives.
- We begin to trust and act on our own instincts.
- We are being sincere, creative, and more self-reliant.

We are on track when we acknowledge that we long to know:

- What is more important than being an emotional child?
- What truth about myself should I trust more?
- What might I discover by giving myself what I need?
- What would it be like to have all the answers to my own questions?
- How do I stop contributing to rage legacies of fear, helplessness, self-loathing, and abuse of the feminine?

DEPRESSION DISGUISE OF RAGE

We know we wear the *Depression* disguise of rage when we have a life pattern of being unhappy. This disguise of rage is not to be confused with the depression we may feel during various life challenges of acute loss. Situational depression, especially if prolonged, generally has biological implications or may represent a chemical imbalance in the brain, requiring medication or other professional support. The *Depression* disguise of rage is more characteristic of a lifestyle in which we have conditioned ourselves to stamp out all evidence of rage. But along with stamping out all rage, we also extinguish any light and optimism, and without light we feel downhearted, detached, sad, and hopeless. Needless to say, these are painful and despairing tradeoffs.

We are likely to live as shut-ins. We find it difficult to take care of our emotional and physical health. Even when money is not an issue, we tend to collapse when it comes to caring for ourselves. We may have trouble taking care of practical needs like vehicle maintenance, paying bills, or caring for our bodies. We are vulnerable to illnesses that catch us off guard and incapacitate us for long periods of time. Our conversations with others are often about our fatigue or misery, which we are capable of articulating in elaborate detail. Those closest to us often must accommodate our unhappiness.

While we are overwhelmed by our problems, we become deeply upset when it seems like others don't have confidence in us. We complain to others about our troubles then feel undermined by their efforts to help. We want to be rescued yet any rescue attempt confirms our fear of being perceived as needy or incompetent. We often can't face dealing with other people. When around others, we don't always have much to say. Speaking takes effort and draws too much attention to us, neither of which are comfortable experiences. While we don't mind engaging, we are less likely to initiate it or be able to maintain it.

We prefer time alone where we can do whatever we want, have time to think, and dream without ridicule. We don't like the idea of anyone watching us. To be watched is to be judged. We tend to have a strong and vivid internal landscape. We are generally creative and have hidden talents, but we lack confidence in our ability to express or negotiate our needs, and we will often sabotage our potential by avoiding risks.

When we can, we sleep to avoid the hassles of living. We may use drugs and alcohol to help blur our thoughts, numb our despair, and help us fall asleep. We have tendencies toward panic attacks, phobias, and social anxiety. We mentally punish ourselves for the mere suggestion of taking a risk, saying to ourselves: *I've tried that already. This won't work. Nobody cares. I'm too tired.* We are capable but we feel either over- or underwhelmed. We are paralyzed with negativity and hopelessness, and resent the demands life imposes—even those we impose on ourselves.

Depression is our way of shrinking in physical and emotional size to silence the rage we feel for existing. We hide from others, including ourselves. Relationships are avoided because they force engagement and intimacy—both areas of pain and difficulty. We are afraid of the emotional pain, humiliation, and loss that accompany intimacy. At the same time, we are at war with those parts of ourselves that are terrified of becoming sealed off, isolated, unknown, and therefore unloved. We may become sexual to feel alive and to have contact, but the feeling is temporary and often distracts us from a more intimate experience with life. We struggle with our desire to be open enough to be seen and understood while contending with feelings of shame about our depression and physical ills. We often feel like imposters, yet we want to be seen without feeling ashamed and endangered.

While we are highly intelligent, we lack the self-confidence to acknowledge our needs and we lack the ability to ask for what we want. We tend to lose interest and willpower when it becomes necessary to stand up for ourselves. It is common for us to feel extremely tired, even ill, just before we have important work to do, and especially when we have to do things we don't want to do. We will often feel disappointed and betrayed, and become frustrated when others fail to recognize and promote our well-being. In our brooding, we hope to be discovered over our deeper desire to be bold and daring. We ultimately feel ashamed of both failing and *feeling* like a failure. However, a caring sign from others, even a stranger, can give us hope.

When others complain, we feel guilty, as if we are at fault. We detest the expectations others have of us. To avoid conflict we accommodate their needs, and resent them and ourselves for it. Then we try to disappear or become unavailable. While we want to defend ourselves, we do not want to be challenged or confronted, or held to others' standards. The rage rules we insist on in most relationships are:

Depression Rule #1: Don't humiliate me by expecting me to share what I feel!
Depression Rule #2: Don't force me to take risks!
Depression Rule #3: Don't smother or overwhelm me!
Depression Rule #4: Don't disregard or ignore me!
Depression Rule #5: Don't look at me too closely!

When others break these rage rules, we rarely explode. Our first instinct is to withdraw and isolate, but we will do what is expected because we often feel in a bind, responsible to do as we are told and what is expected of us. But we hate it. At times we feel unbearably alone and afraid. We shut down our feelings in an attempt to deaden our pain. We feel sorry for ourselves and may even become preoccupied more with death than with life. We are ashamed that we need to be discovered and rescued from our despair, and worse, we banish anyone who tries to support us. Those of us wearing the *Depression* disguise generally fall short of seriously harming ourselves physically; however, some of us may inflict injuries to our bodies to alter our mood.

Wearing the *Depression* disguise means that as children, we lived in despair and could not fathom the traumas we experienced, nor have we grieved them. We found it difficult to get positive, support-ive, affectionate attention from our caretakers. We thought that if we became sick or surrendered to our despair, we would be sure to be rescued, but we weren't. Even when sick or needy, we often felt we had to care for ourselves. It was then that we convinced ourselves that nothing we did made a difference. Since then, we have negotiated with life moment to moment—deciding whether to live out loud or in hiding. Despite our dark thoughts and feelings, we choose to live. In fact, we make amazing things happen in our lives, often behind the scenes. We choose to live yet we derive little joy from living.

A DAY IN THE LIFE OF AGNES—*DEPRESSION*

I hate my job more than ever since they didn't give me that promotion last week. I'm good at what I do and the kids I work with like me. What's the problem? Okay, I don't have a high need to be social with folks. But that's not why they pay me.

The head of the residential program always chooses me to do those art projects. My colleagues are jealous so they avoid me. Right after they told me I wouldn't be promoted, I spoke up in a meeting. It wasn't easy and my thoughts were not very clear, but I managed to get it out. A colleague exploded telling me I complained too much. I was enraged and thought to my-self: "I knew I shouldn't have said anything. It goes to show you, speaking up is pointless. Nothing can be changed. Why bother." I didn't say anything. I just dealt with it silently and was relieved when we moved on to discuss the next agenda item. But I couldn't wait to disappear after the meeting.

Another colleague told me I should have stood up for my-self. It's true. I didn't speak up. But, guess what—it doesn't make any difference! Nothing does. Nobody seems to notice or care. Why didn't anyone else stand up for me? I know why, because they're all too lame, weak, and stupid. But who am I to criticize them? I am the lamest, weakest, and stupidest of all. Besides, how could I expect them to care if my own husband didn't? He filed for divorce and told everyone I was a complete bore. He seemed to enjoy showing off his new pregnant girlfriend to everyone. He had no idea how devastating this was to me after twelve years of marriage. He got his divorce and a new life. What did I get? Nothing.

My mom worries about me and my kids. She thinks I'm stuck and need therapy. She's been telling me this all my life. She also thinks I should move back home and start fresh. I listen to her and don't say much. The more I tell her, the more meddlesome she becomes. Some of her ideas are good, but it's my life. Hell, I'm too tired to worry about that. Besides, I hate it when others expect me to do more. I just get as far away from them as possible.

Everybody thinks they know what's best for me. I don't understand it. They seem angry and more emotional about my life than I am. Why can't they see what I'm doing? I'm good at what I do and I work hard keeping things together, yet they seem to easily blow my world apart with their worries and expectations. They say they are trying to help me, but I don't feel helped. I feel invisible, controlled, and intruded upon. I avoid them because they only make me feel worse about myself. Considering everything I'm going through, it's amazing I'm doing as well as I am. I know I'm angry about all this, but I'm just not feeling it.

After working that dead-end job all day and running around town picking up the kids, I'm exhausted. We rarely do anything in the evenings and on weekends—I'm too tired. Sometimes I sleep on and off all day. I wake up exhausted and try to grab sleep wherever I can. The kids get stir crazy and on my nerves, but I've taught the ten-year-old to care for the two-year-old so I can get some sleep. It's not their fault I'm tired, but I just can't do anything else. Thank God for TV and takeout.

But it's always been this way. Nothing I do is appreciated. I don't want to stop living but it often feels more attractive than dragging around. The only reason I keep functioning is because I have to—I have to work, so I do. I have to pick up the kids, so I do. I had to divorce, so I did. But that's it. It seems impossible for me to do the things I really want to do. Most of the time I'm just holding on. But I'm afraid that one day, I'll just come to a dead stop, and that will be it—the end. And worse, no one will notice or care. Last night I got really scared, like something bad was going to happen to me, like I might even hurt myself. I think I was having an anxiety attack. I didn't know what to do. I just knew I needed help.

JOURNALING QUESTIONS

1. What thoughts, feelings, memories, or sensations did you experience while reading about *Depression*?
2. What aspect of this disguise is alive in your life?
3. Who or what does this disguise remind you of?
4. What does *Depression* teach you about rage and the need to heal?

THE WISDOM OF DEPRESSION—SOLITUDE

To survive, we have plumbed the depths of sorrow and shame and we know the courage needed to travel there. Our deep waters are a well from which great creativity is drawn. We have a highly attuned ability to discern profound meaning in ways that move the human heart. When the fear and shame that has compelled us begins to lift, our unique insight and counsel can be brought to generous and spontaneous light. Our knowledge of the human heart allows us to naturally empathize with others and to be a wise and intimate friend.

LETTING GO

We are beginning to let go of the *Depression* disguise of rage when we notice that:

- We are shifting from feeling isolated and hopeless to becoming more invested in the quality of our lives and life itself.
- When we are not hiding behind the scenes but being the main character of our lives.
- When we can ask for what we want and be determined to have it.

We are on track when we acknowledge that we long to know:

- Why have I chosen to live?
- What is worth living for?
- Who am I if I let go of my despair?
- What can I create that speaks louder than words?
- How do I stop contributing to rage legacies of despair, dispiritedness, and self-abuse?

PART THREE

Inner-Peace
Practices

7

Preparing for the Journey

Sacred Practices

It is not rage that harms us—it is our entrapment in the disguises we wear. Disguises are like an intricate work of art, a piece of armor sewn deep into our emotions and our nervous systems, carefully created by a very young part of ourselves determined to live. Having constructed and worn these disguises for our very survival, we have been deeply shaped by them and they are likely to be with us throughout our lives, emerging most strongly at times when we feel threatened.

Our fear and shame of our raw experiences of rage keep us from climbing into our hearts and becoming whole, yet when the compulsion that drove us to wear our disguise is lifted, the shape that is left behind will often reveal our deepest yearnings and our greatest strengths.

There are worlds of experience and ways of being that lie beyond the habits of our conditioning. In the following chapters, we will discover that we are not our disguises—we are much more. We will learn how to examine the clever construction of our intricate disguises with compassion. We will celebrate those parts of ourselves that we have acknowledged, and embrace those parts we have disowned. We will experience the impermanence of rage and live more fully in the present moment. We will discover that we can wear our disguises less often and more lightly, like a loose robe rather than a suit of armor grafted onto our skin, and even learn to lay them aside so that a new curiosity or expanded truth can emerge. The wisdom of rage is fuel—already on fire within us, and these fierce energies have the power to wake us up, transform our lives, and create legacies that liberate the heart.

We begin by placing rage into its natural habitat—an elemental realm—like a season we anticipate and prepare for, rather than a problem we avoid, get a grip on, or try to change. In its natural form, rage simply *is*—neutral, neither good nor bad.

Rage is energy that arises from thought and registers as sensation in the body. In this regard, rage is information—mail delivered that has not been read or translated; an inner fire that flares under predictable circumstances. Rage has healing properties that, when nurtured, help us understand, expand, and mobilize our life's purpose. As we grow wise in our ability to attend lovingly to rage as a sacred messenger, we naturally heal from its warmth and insight. Our challenge is in knowing how to utilize the energies of rage for our own transformation.

At a professional conference on the East Coast, I presented a keynote address on healing rage to women psychologists and asked the audience: *How much time do you spend fighting issues of oppression?* They were confident in their responses. One woman said: *I've spent most of my life fighting racism!* Another one piped in: *I spend too much of my time fighting sexism and homophobia.* We had twenty minutes of voluntary responses to this question, each one topping the previous one. Then I asked them to consider: *What do you imagine you would feel in the absence of oppression? Who would you be if you were not at war? If you were to stop fighting, what would you be doing with your time? What vision do you have of victory? Does your vi-*

sion include peace within yourself and throughout the world? An awkward silence fell across the room, as if an unspoken pact had somehow been violated. One woman spoke her thoughts out loud: *I'd lose a big part of my identity if I stopped fighting, and that frightens me.* This brave woman is describing the terror inherent in giving up a disguise of rage. In such a moment it is difficult to grasp that acknowledging such truth is the literal experience of transforming—what makes inner peace possible.

We may not always experience peace, but peace is always present—it is the white space between the black letters on this page. Peace has to do with where we place our attention. I recall an early winter morning while on a month-long silent retreat. In the middle of the meditation, a rainstorm rocked the hall. I noticed thoughts of anger keeping beat with the rain because I had left my umbrella in my bedroom several buildings away. I became obsessed with worry— *Damn, I'll get soaked going back to my room. I didn't bring the right clothes for a storm. I'm going to miss breakfast if I have to go all the way back to my room, and there won't be any food left for me, and I'm starving—so hungry I could die. How I could make such a stupid mistake, anyway?*

What I did wrong and the resulting *something bad will now happen to me* was all I could think about. My thoughts became so intense I opened my eyes. There before me sat a woman with a soft, pleasing smile on her face, as if she was enjoying the sound of rain thundering through the hall. It occurred to me that rain was what was really happening, and a more peaceful point of focus than my more punishing thoughts of not having an umbrella. Whenever we find ourselves obsessing on thoughts or worry, consider what peace we may be missing in the present moment.

Not only is inner peace possible, it is ever-present and accessible when we can put rage in sacred perspective. This does not mean we never experience rage or other difficult emotions. Rather we can awaken to how peace lives within and is always an available option, albeit one that is foreign to many of us. Not being peaceful is a habit we formed when our focus was more on surviving. It is a habit that can be broken with a practice of self-love.

The process of healing rage is different for each person. Yet it is common for the process to trigger the *Rage/Shame Duo*, and a tug-of-war can erupt in our body and mind. For example, rage wants to come out into the open and tell its story, while shame wants to hide our stories and be safe from danger. As we disrobe our disguises of rage and move closer to ourselves, we may experience a range of emotions that belong to the shame family—fear, ambivalence, help-lessness, confusion, grief, sorrow, regret, obliviousness, innocence, and, at times, nothing at all. It is also possible that we might experi-ence moments of insecurity, hypersensitivity, or agitation.

While the fires of rage can be illuminating, our rage child is best understood in the context of a sacred practice of contemplative self-witnessing, where we can examine our feelings and actions in relative quiet and introspection. A sacred practice allows us to cultivate our deepest intentions of kindness and well-being, and support us in re-garding ourselves and all that is around us with respect. If we want peace in the world, we must practice peace. The operative word is *practice*—becoming aware of how we live true to our intentions and beliefs. The following practices are offered to prepare you for your healing journey. These preparatory practices will be expanded in later chapters. For now, integrate them into your daily awareness.

KEEPING A RAGE JOURNAL

It will be useful to maintain a rage journal to record your experi-ences. Find a journal that you can carry with you for easy access. As a daily practice, record your feelings and thoughts. Some have found it helpful to record their thoughts at the same time each day. Write down the date and time of each entry. Start with writing a half page each time you record. You may want to expand over time.

Use all of your senses and capture the details of your experiences as clearly and colorfully as possible. Don't inhibit your expression. Draw a picture or symbol, write a poem, or scribble random words. Most importantly, don't edit what you write. After you write on the pages, simply close your journal until the next day. No one should read your journal unless you choose to share it. Throughout this book you will be invited to journal and review what you have written. For now, keep your journal and favorite pen ready!

SETTING SACRED INTENTION

To cultivate a sacred practice with rage, we must be willing to let go of our misery, remember what we love about ourselves, and know why we are here. Our rage child endangers our mind, body, and spirit when we betray ourselves—live untrue to our spirit. She knows that we are much more than our past experiences and the disguises we wear to hide them. Our very life is a path of awakening. When we explore the deeper reasons we are here, we put rage in sacred perspective and open to the light of its wisdom. Ponder the following questions, or feel free to use these questions as a journaling exercise:

1. Do I live true to myself?
2. In what do I place my faith?
3. What values do I live by?
4. What do I love more than I fear?
5. What is worth dying for? Living for?
6. If I knew the date of my death, how would it change how I live?
7. What is my life here to heal?
8. What do my ancestors require of me?
9. How do I live in a way that brings out the best of who I am?
10. How do I use my life to bring goodness into the world?
11. What vision do I have of inner and world peace?
12. How will I know when I am peaceful?

Ask yourself these questions with genuine curiosity. The mere asking invokes a dance with spirit that reveals deeper meaning. Don't expect to have the answers immediately. Rather, allow them to reveal themselves to you in any number of surprising, even auspicious ways—in your significant relationships, disagreements, quiet times, or with strangers, newborns, elders, teenagers, animals, nature, or in your dreams. Also, don't be surprised if you find yourself answering the questions again and again as you deepen your inquiry. The idea is not to have fixed answers but rather to enjoy the dance of inquiry.

CREATING A SACRED SPACE

Just as we may prepare a nursery or special space for a newborn, it is important that you create a space where you welcome your rage child and begin to notice and honor yourself. In this space, you become aware of how your disguises of rage interfere with your sacred intentions, and how to parent yourself like no one else can.

You may already have such a space or practice of contemplation. If so, include your intention to heal rage. If not, create or designate a space—a room or the corner of a room, basement, attic, or even a closet. Personalize this space to your liking with colors, textures, and other items that your rage child might enjoy. Be creative yet purposeful in designing your space. Use whatever works for you. Blanche didn't have a space in the apartment she shared with five other people, but she did take a bath each morning, which became her sacred space with her rage child. She tossed in a rubber duck as a symbol of her rage child and spent a few minutes being mindful of her thoughts and setting an intention of self-care for the day.

If it is not possible to locate a space inside your home, look in your neighborhood for a mature tree, a body of water, or some other peaceful and private place. Wherever you decide to establish your sacred space, make sure it is clean, private, welcoming, and easily accessible. You will want to return to this space regularly. Eventually, you will naturally carry this space within. Any act of self-awareness is a step in the direction of healing rage.

When you enter your sacred space, shift your attention to your healing. Just as when you enter a church, temple, mosque, or synagogue, the same reverence should be given to your sacred place. You may want to begin with a prayer, bow, chant, poem, mantra, song, or spontaneous greeting of respect. You may light a candle or burn a scent. Every action should be mindful, carrying the spirit of love and the intentions of goodwill, discovery, and peace. These intentional acts of kindness toward rage bring warmth and inner peace.

PREPARING A RAGE ALTAR

Within your sacred space, you may want to spread a cloth or have a small table that holds items of significance to you on this journey. Some people refer to this as an altar. Altars have been used for thousands of years in many religious and spiritual practices as useful and pleasing focal points of devotion. Ancestors, family, abundance— anything that you want to keep in your awareness is often worthy of a special place to focus your intention.

Creating a *Rage Altar* is a mindful gesture to welcome your rage child and affirm your intention to be aware of your healing journey. A rage altar can include items of significance to your rage child's history or items that symbolize your rage inheritance, spiritual or religious practice, ancestors, or culture. For example, Delores placed old pictures of herself on her altar next to a picture of Jesus and a childhood birthday card from her mother. Lisa chose to spread a sacred cloth from Israel, a gift from her great-grandmother, as the surface of her altar for rage, and placed baby pictures of herself and her great-grandmother on the cloth. Debra had a pair of bronze baby shoes and a small jar of hair barrettes similar to the ones she wore as a child. Denise's altar contained an image of the Buddha, a picture of herself, and pictures of her family with whom she hoped to reunite.

Should you choose to have a rage altar, you may also want to place on it items from each of four elements—fire, water, air, and earth. For instance, you may light a white candle to represent the spirit of your rage child, ancestors, and the spirits of all those suffering with rage throughout the world. A clear glass of salt or ocean water can symbolize your tears and those of the world from lost innocence, grief, sorrow, and pain. Water can awaken your subconscious and unconscious mind and reveal your purest longings. Air is most symbolized by your breath and may also include incense or fragrances that can inspire spiritual clarity. Rocks, an earth element, can symbolize the bones of your ancestors and can absorb and hold your pain and power. Consider other natural objects as well. Prior to placing any item on your altar or within your sacred space, hold it close to your heart and speak its purpose and your intention.

The idea of an altar is not to make it perfect, but to make it purposeful—a focal point symbolic of your intention to heal. Your intention is what is most important. Don't worry if something does not immediately come to mind. Trust your rage child to inform you of what is needed. Your rage altar will develop naturally over time.

THE *BEING NOW* MANTRA

The *Being Now* mantra is a mental phrase that when repeated invites the body to respond. Here is the mantra: *Deep Breaths, Soft Belly, Open Heart.* The breath always lives in the present moment, and becoming aware of your breath brings you to *Now.* Softening your belly has a grounding effect and makes you aware that you live in your body. Opening your heart invites the entire body to relax and gracefully soften. This harmonizing trio invites your mind and body to join in *Being Now*—being one. Here's how it works:

Take several deep breaths to calm yourself. As you breathe, temporarily suspend your thoughts and feelings. Let your thoughts float like distant clouds. Let your feelings flow like a gentle river. You may say quietly, *I'm okay right now. It's all right now. I'm safe.* Let go as you breathe. Second, allow your belly to soften. As you breathe, bring your awareness into your belly and rest in your core—the space between your belly button and lower back. Breathe from this place and allow your entire body to soften. Finally, focus on the warmth of your heart and allow your heart to open gently like the soft petals of a rose on a sunny day. With each inhalation and exhalation, let your chest become spacious, warm, and more relaxed. Continue breathing in this full-bodied way.

Repeat this mantra throughout the day as often as you can remember it—for example, when you are washing your hands, sitting down to eat, showering, driving, cooking, at the top of the hour, prior to meditating, or prior to speaking. Whatever you are doing, begin to condition your mind and body to listen to and comply with these words.

STARTING A *STILLNESS PRACTICE*

A *Stillness Practice* is a daily routine of self-noticing that prepares the mind for peace. We are already aware, wise, and peaceful—we only need to be still and experience it. Rage is intensified by our confusion and terror, and becomes less intense as we witness and welcome "what is" without distraction, resistance, or over-identification. This requires that we make stillness a practice.

It is best to practice at the same time each day and in the same location—your sacred space. You might begin with ten minutes per sitting twice a day and increase your time as you experience the calm inherent in this practice. It is not important how long you sit but rather how consistently you practice. To begin, sit comfortably and quietly in your sacred space, undisturbed, with your eyes gently closed. Begin by relaxing into the *Being Now* mantra. That's it!

If you have young children and find it difficult to get away for ten minutes, have your children practice with you. Teach them the practice of stillness. Stillness is a natural state. Alice told her four-year-old twins, *Come and sit with mommy. It feels good to be quiet. We can sit and be still like angels. Watch me, and do what I do. Breathe. Close your eyes. And no talking! Okay? When you hear the bell, we will go and have breakfast!* Of course, the twins didn't always follow the rules, but they became accustomed to the routine, and while they didn't always sit still, they learned not to talk or disturb Alice after a while. One of the twins began to enjoy the practice and was more consistent. Your example and sharing of the practice of stillness is a profound yet inexpensive gift for the young people in your life.

A daily practice of stillness allows us to calm our mind and rest in our body. We condition ourselves to be present in our experiences without being controlled by them. We will build on this *Stillness Practice* and learn about meditating in later chapters in this book. For now, just get into the habit of practicing stillness each day.

RECORDING YOUR DREAMS

Our intention to heal often encourages our rage child to reveal herself in our dreams. The dream world is a safe haven for our rage child because she can be outrageous and creative without our conscious control, while also enticing us to seek understanding of her rage riddles. A rage riddle is a story that is imbedded in our dreams that invites us to decode its message and better understand our lives. There is tremendous rage wisdom embedded in our dreams, but we must first strive to remember and record them.

Just before going to sleep, ask your spirit guides to help you wake up, remember, and write down your dreams. Keep a rage journal next to your bed. When you awake, write your dreams as if you are still in them. It does not matter if you do not remember every detail. What you do remember is what is important. Simply write what you are seeing, thinking, doing, and feeling in the dream *in the present tense.*

I write on the right-side pages of my journal, saving the opposite pages for later interpretations. Most importantly, don't change, interpret, or judge what is occurring in your dream, or edit what you are writing. Later we will explore how to interpret rage riddles in dreams. For now, just get your dream on paper!

Healing is the process of becoming more self-aware. We unfold, let go, and discover who we are—who we have always been. We dignify rage when we honor the truth, and we begin by *re*-membering ourselves— looking back to understand our present, then moving forward.

8

Re-Membering—
Looking Back to Move Forward

Now that we have put our rage child in sacred perspective, we can turn our attention to *re*-membering the childhood traumas that gave birth to our rage. *Re*-membering is similar to being an anthropologist, where we excavate or uncover our inner rage experiences to become reacquainted with our fuller selves. This inner history is more accessible to us now that we have begun to put aside our rage disguises and commit ourselves to a relationship with rage.

The first time I led a group of women to Egypt in a journey of *re*-membrance, I recall standing in the inner chamber of the Temple of Philae—Isis Temple, a few miles upstream from Elephantine—feeling the silent stories of my ancestors echo from the walls. The Egyptologist related the myth of Isis and Osiris. Osiris—a powerful and prosperous king of Skondia in northern Egypt—was murdered by his envious brother, Set, a poor king of southern Egypt. Set not only killed his brother, he dismembered him by cutting him into fourteen pieces and scattering his body parts along the whole length of the Nile, hoping the crocodiles would devour them, leaving him to rule. I'm intrigued that it was Osiris's *body* that was dismembered, for it was his physical wholeness that was most feared by his brother. Osiris's mutilation and scattering was intended to strip him of his power. Death alone was not enough. Keeping his body parts separate was a sure way to control his spirit from returning.

Isis, Osiris's beloved wife, a powerful queen and healer, took years to gather his scattered body parts, and she was 99 percent successful. The quick-and-dirty version of the story, I'm told, is that she was unable to locate his penis, so she constructed one of wood, made love to him, and Osiris's spiritual life was conceived in the form of a son, Horus, who grew up to become a king and avenge the wrongs done to his father.

Egyptian mythology is full of mystery and symbolism, requiring years of understanding to decipher its complex meaning. Yet I could not help but wonder, at times humorously, about the absence of the legitimate voice of rage. While the Egyptologist focused on the heroics, I found myself mentally filling in the gaps—the good king dies at the hand of the bad king for the good of his kingdom. It must have been traumatic for Osiris to be manipulated and murdered by his brother and cut to pieces. I can only imagine his terror and helplessness as he lay captive facing his demise. But *what about Isis?* I would think that she was enraged that she lost the love of her life in such a brutal way, and that it took her years to repossess his scattered pieces. And a penis of wood? Talk about the short end of the stick! Who wouldn't be enraged about that!

Making fun of a sacred tale is a cheap shot, yet it makes this point: The most authentic voice one could have in situations like this is rage. Yet as women, for our survival we have depended on both silencing and denying our rage—being politically correct and socially heroic while becoming physically exhausted, emotionally disconnected yet desperate, and spiritually bankrupt.

It's not difficult to understand why we would be afraid to *re-*member ourselves. *Re-*membering evokes feelings of helplessness, anxiety, pain, and shame—emotions that trigger rage. However, we are all Osiris—powerful and innately prosperous, yet traumatized by fear and ignorance and affected by the needs of others to violate and control our body and our lives. Uncountable parts of ourselves have been dismembered—cut off, lost, and scattered along the paths of our lives. Consequently, we have learned how to live without all of our parts. We are all Isis—the beloved healer, capable of *re*-membering ourselves: gathering our lost parts and bringing ourselves back to physical, emotional, and spiritual wholeness, and even able to bring about a blessing in the form of continuation.

Isis was perhaps one of the first anthropologists, aka healer of rage. I'm guessing that she approached her work of *re*-membering very mindfully, careful not to destroy or dismiss any of her discoveries. Similarly, our intent in *re*-membering is not to deny, destroy, or dismiss the details of our memories, but rather to reassemble our history and liberate ourselves from shame and fear to wholeness.

We unearth the pieces of our past not to feel bad or dwell on the horrific details, but rather to examine our traumas *and* how we have come to respond to them. For this task we use an *Empathic Inquiry* to help us *re*-member our traumatic experiences of childhood and to make an explicit agreement with ourselves to put to rest what is already behind us.

EMPATHIC INQUIRY

Take a few weeks to complete the following exercise, allowing plenty of time to *re*-member and reflect on your childhood (up to the age of twelve years). You may want to devote your daily *Stillness Practice* to this task in your sacred space, or respond to these questions whenever the answers make themselves known.

Read all of the questions below before you respond to them. When you are ready, record your answers in your journal without edit or review. Write as much detail as you can recall. If it becomes difficult to write your responses, write about the difficulty you are having.

It is not necessary that you have a complete recollection of your childhood experiences—this would be impossible. It does not matter if what you recall is the absolute truth. It is also not necessary for you to maintain a balanced view, weighing in all the good things your childhood offered. What matters is that through this exercise, you will see the relationship between your past and the present—what you have continued to live even though you thought you left it behind.

Feel free to ignore questions that do not apply, or add questions that you have about your childhood and respond to them as well. You are on a sacred journey, which means much will be revealed. Don't be alarmed if you find yourself recording answers to questions you have not verbally asked. Relax into your *Being Now* mantra. Allow your heart and mind to flow naturally onto your journal pages.

EMPATHIC QUESTIONNAIRE

1. What were the circumstances that surrounded your birth (emotional, political, cultural, social, economical, parental, etc.)?
2. What is your sweetest memory as a child?
3. When did you realize you were special? That you weren't? How did you know?
4. Who were your role models when you were young? Why?
5. What was most important to you as a child? Why?
6. When did your heart first start to close? Why?
7. What did you love most about your father? Your mother? Your caretaker(s)?
8. What pains you deeply to remember?
9. What were you accused of doing that you didn't do?
10. What did you learn about love as a child? From whom did you learn it?
11. What values did you gain as a child from your parents/ guardians that help you most in life?

12. What was your earliest experience of letting go? Of being let go of?
13. What happened that should not have happened?
14. What did you want to change but couldn't?
15. What was your greatest loss, failure, disappointment, or misfortune?
16. What physical, emotional, or mental illnesses or anguish do you recall having? How often did you have them?
17. What were you most ashamed of? Most enraged about?
18. What did you have to be an adult about when you were a child?
19. What story can you tell now that you couldn't tell then?
20. What elder/ancestor had the most impact on you as a child? Why?

A *LIFE LINE* TO *RE*-MEMBER

Another way to explore your childhood experiences is through a *Life Line* exercise (diagram below). The *Life Line* is a visual way of recalling your experiences. Here's how it works:

Draw a horizontal line across the middle of a large piece of paper. The space above the line represents positive experiences, whereas the space below the line represents negative experiences.

On the left end of the line, put a 0 indicating your birth, and at the opposite end put a 12, which represents the end of your childhood (or you can go out as far as you like). Indicate the emotional highs and lows of your childhood experiences for each point that corresponds to your ages or the memorable points of your life. You may complete this *Life Line* exercise before you journal your responses to the *Empathic Questionnaire*, or after.

Once you have completed these tasks to your satisfaction, put what you have written aside for a few hours or days. Many feelings emerge when we are *re*-membering our rage, and it is important to

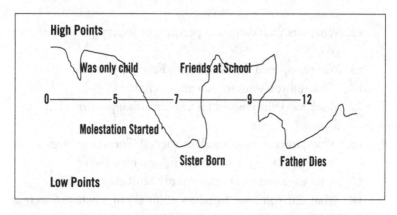

take care of ourselves along the way. If you find yourself feeling over-whelmed by what you are discovering, take a break and let what you know rest in your heart before moving forward. Healing rage is a journey of compassionate self-awareness, not a specific destination. There is no rush—this is a life's work!

UNDERSTANDING YOUR RAGE MEMOIRS

When you are ready, read what you have written slowly and without judgment or criticism, then ponder these questions:

- How do you feel about what you have written?
- What can you celebrate about your survival?
- What still frightens you? Saddens you? Shames you? Enrages you? Why?
- What seems unbelievable? Absolute? Questionable?
- What deal did you make with yourself back then that you still live with today, i.e., via disguises?
- How is your rage today similar to your mother's? Your father's? Your ancestors'? Your culture's?
- What part of your childhood interferes with your healing?
- What other insights can you glean from this exercise?

When you are done, put aside your journal and sit quietly in stillness. Allow some time to go by before you review what you have written. It takes tremendous courage to address the answers to these questions, and a break is well earned. Do something nice for yourself: take a warm bath, get a massage, take a walk in nature, read a juicy romance novel, watch a comedy movie, or spend time with a healthy lover or an uncomplicated friend. The important thing is not to discuss this exercise with anyone, at least for now. Just take a break and allow what you have uncovered to rest and settle within you.

When you are ready, return to your rage journal and review what you have written. Uprooting childhood traumas may evoke emotions. You may feel and remember what you once knew, and reexperience the traumas that made it necessary for you to hide within your disguises. You may experience a deepening, for example, as you feel the difference between your mind *knowing* the truth and your body physically *experiencing* the truth. Or you may find you had one experience writing and another reading what you wrote. When we read our journals, we will often *feel* what we know. This is because the act of writing—finding the right words and adhering to sentence structure—uses our intellect. But when reading what we wrote our emotions are freer to react. All in all, our fierce truth, although long suppressed and misunderstood, is still active and waiting to be liberated.

Re-membering allows us to gently excavate those parts of our past that are hidden, denied, forgotten, and even deplorable, and bring them to light and new meaning. The events of our lives are not mistakes. They have profoundly shaped who we are. All of our experiences are teaching us how to live in outrageous dignity. Take honorable notice!

9

Entertaining Wildness

THE RAGE RELEASE RITUAL

As we continue to disrobe our disguises, our emotions are more readily accessible, yet our understanding and ability to use our rage effectively is still undeveloped. This combination of feeling more but not feeling in control causes anxiety and discomfort.

The most compassionate thing we can do for ourselves at times is to express rage. Think about it this way. Your rage child has recently been released from the prison of your disguises for crimes she did not commit, and her truth is still trapped in your body. She wants her day in court—an opportunity to tell you her version of the story without being silenced, corrected, or polite. She wants to be angry and scream: *This was horrible!* and hear you say, *You're right!* She needs an opportunity to ask: *Why did you hurt me? Why did you leave me?* She wants to share her pain: *This hurts! Please help me! Please protect me! Never abandon me again.* She is that part of you that needs to forgive and be forgiven. A rage release ritual can help us to relieve some of this pressure.

The intention of the rage release ritual is to liberate the pure spirit of rage—to allow your emotions and nervous system to feel release. The goal of the rage release ritual is not simply to blow off steam. With this ritual, you are harmonizing your body and mind without pretense, and allowing yourself to have an authentic experience of rage. You design an experience in which the energies of your rage spirit can be physically released. The idea is to have the experience of completely letting go and losing control in a private and safe space. Energetically, you are creating more inner space to feel more relieved and spacious, to rest momentarily and begin to see and understand yourself more distinctly.

The nature of rage is to engage—to be in contact with something or someone. In many cultures, men are socialized toward high-contact sports, even sexual aggression, both of which can serve as temporary physical and emotional outlets for rage. Quite the opposite, women are socialized to be polite and to serve others. Some women fear that if they release rage verbally and physically it poisons the environs. It is important to know that truth does not harm us—it liberates us. There is nothing we feel that does not already belong to the world and is not in fact a part of the world. For many women, this ritual is the first time in their lives that they can allow themselves to verbally and physically express the full emotional intensity of rage without holding it in, turning it against themselves, or concerning themselves with how someone else feels about it. I have worked with thousands of women, most of whom are absolutely amazed at the breakthrough quality inherent in the physical and verbal release of rage. One woman shares: *Rage is a song I've always sang, just never out loud.*

To heal rage, you must be willing to experience its nature—get close to the heat and be warmed and informed by it. As women, it serves us to understand this part of ourselves to the fullest. Don't worry. Generally, you will need to do this ritual only a few times. It's a way of physically introducing yourself to your rage child. To many, it is like giving birth—you don't like the pain, but you gain so much in return.

The rage release ritual is a powerful way to affirm to yourself that you are capable of physically relieving your own suffering. By no means should you attempt this ritual if you are feeling like you could be a danger to yourself or someone else. If this is the case, seek immediate support from a therapist, crisis hotline, or hospital. There are three conditions you need to accept before proceeding:

1. You are not to physically hurt others or yourself.
2. You are not to destroy property.
3. If you are enraged with a particular person, that person is not present during this ritual. You are not to engage verbally or physically with the person you are enraged with. This time is for you.

This ritual can be practiced as often as needed and especially when you harbor intense feelings or any time you simply want to experiment with inviting your rage child to express her true nature. For example, after completing the *Empathic Questionnaire*, you may want to explode in rage, tears, or both. This would be an excellent time to have a rage release ritual. Other times may include after returning home at the end of a maddening day, or after having a fight with your partner, or after dealing with insane traffic. Most of you do not have to search far for a reason to have a rage release ritual.

Ideally, you will want a space private enough to scream, stomp, curse, cry, shout, kick, rip, roar, and rage! You may want to gather some of the following items:

- A dozen old magazines or telephone books to rip to shreds.
- Several large pillows to pound, scream into, or rest on.
- A large army duffel bag stuffed with old clothes to beat, kick, and punch.
- A belt or a two-foot-long rubber hose for whacking the magazines and beating the duffel bag.
- A large blanket to cover yourself when you want contact.
- A stuffed animal to cuddle with for comfort.

You may need fifteen minutes to an hour for a rage release ritual. If other adults are near, tell them that you may be making some noise, and not to worry. Ask them not to disturb you. Send your kids to a friend's house for a few hours. Send your roommates out for pizza. You need to be able to focus on yourself, and not on other people nearby. You can turn on loud music to encourage the release of rage or to distort your sounds, or you can scream into a pillow. If you cannot get enough privacy at home or in your sacred space, you can take a walk in an open space or drive your car to a private and safe place.

A word of caution: Do not drive while you are out of control with rage. Instead, pull over and let it rip! Automobiles are safe portable containers for rage as long as they are not moving and you do not hurt yourself in the confined space.

A word of encouragement: The more release, the more relief. You are hereby authorized to *"tear the roof off the . . ."* Don't try to be fair, reasonable, or rational during your rage release. It does not matter if what you are saying makes sense or is the truth or a lie. What's important is that you say it—all of it. Be *out*raged: *I fucked up, again! He raped me! That bitch didn't pay me back! He's an asshole! She disrespected me! I hate paying these damn bills! They refused my apology! After all I've done, they fired me! I hate you! I'm sick and tired of being sick and tired! I love you, damn it! He slept with my best friend! She left me! I hate myself!* Whatever!

There is no right way to have a rage release ritual. The idea is to release your rage physically and verbally, rest in the inner space you've created, and deepen your understanding of rage. The process involves the following steps:

1. Retreat to your sacred space and affirm to your rage child that this is her time to come out. Reassure her that you will not harm yourself or others.
2. Invite your sacred spirits to witness and support you in a full release of raging truth.
3. Standing or sitting, take several deep breaths and begin to recall

and speak out loud your incident of rage in vivid and righteous detail. Start softly, and let your voice become louder and louder. It is important to engage your voice in this exercise—to break silence.

4. Allow your rage child to have her way—exploding out of your body and mind—and let her loose! Use any of the materials at hand—ripping paper, beating on the duffel bag, stomping, and screaming. Let her rip!

5. Once you are done releasing rage, wrap yourself in a blanket and rock yourself gently. It is common to cry following a rage release. The *Rage/Shame Duo* is at play, and whenever rage is present, shame follows. The reverse is also true, so don't be surprised if you are resting or crying and want to rage again. Allow that natural dance of rage and shame to unfold.

6. When you have settled, rest with your stuffed animal as you mentally thank your spirit guides, ancestors, and rage child for their support. Practice *Being Now.* Tell yourself that you are healing, and that you are precious and brave. You may even want to take a nap.

When you have rested enough, light a candle, take several deep breaths, and take a few moments to write about this experience in your rage journal. As you journal your experiences from your rage release rituals, write down in full detail what you discovered about your rage child. For example, what did she feel like inside your body? What did she feel like coming out of your body? Describe her size, shape, taste, smell, color, gender, and age. Did she change during your release? What was she saying? What was she doing? What did you discover about her pain? What stories did she tell? What did she want? What was she enraged about? What was she afraid of? What was she ashamed of? Does she have a name? If you were to describe her as an artistic expression, what would it be? Capture these reflections and any other key details about your experience in your rage journal as clearly and in as much detail as possible.

After your ritual, expect to feel a bit vulnerable and tender. Try to arrange things so that you have some time alone, without needing to explain yourself or focus too much on the needs of others. Also, be patient with the people around you.

Don't worry if during your ritual you don't do what you had planned, or you don't feel what you expected to feel. Edith's release was only tears. Barbara mumbled like an infant and could not speak words. Deborah never stopped screaming. Alice's ritual was full of elaborate goddess-like gestures, all in silence. Many women wonder if they have done it right, but there is no right way or right outcome from a release. Patricia shares:

> I really didn't buy into all this. I didn't think for one minute that if I followed these suggestions I'd actually have a release of rage. Was I surprised! I started off being upset about how silenced and stuck I felt in my dead-end job. I walked around in my room cursing and blaming folks at work. I then started stomping and I found my lips mimicking my mother who used to say to me as a child: "The military takes good care of us so shut up and be grateful!" And before I knew it, I was raging at her and every other SOB who felt they had a right to silence me. And it felt great! Afterward, I felt lighthearted and tired, but also clear. I regained the strength I needed to defend myself. When I later read what I had written in my journal, I realized that my job was similar to my childhood, only this time, I could complain, and I could also leave. I've always known this, but now I feel this truth in my body and can act on it.

A rage release ritual is often an experience of relief and discovery. Try not to be critical of how your rage child chose to reveal herself.

Keep in mind that the rage release ritual is not a dress rehearsal for you to eventually go out into the world and confront your targets of rage. Most immediately, you are the primary beneficiary of your rage release ritual because you are the one who is healing. Many have discovered that their rage release ritual has provided them with enough calm that they no longer needed to have direct confrontations with others.

DISCOVERING THE CHARACTER OF RAGE

Once you have experienced two to three rage release rituals, you can begin to discern the character of your rage child. Read through your journal entries and consider the following questions:

1. What is your rage child's name and age?
2. Where does she typically live in your body?
3. What circumstances provoke her most actively?
4. How does she make herself known?
5. What is her most common story or upset?
6. What does she want you to know?
7. What does she want you to do for her? Be specific.

As you continue to practice releasing rage, you open to an experience of yourself that is larger than the stories you tell yourself. For instance, you may experience something old in a new way, or experience something you never dreamed of. The point is to become self-aware, and to allow new vitality to flow into the parts of you that are now open.

We begin to heal by acknowledging that rage is tied to our need for self-compassion and our longing to be free from suffering. The physical and verbal release of rage is not an end in itself. The deeper truth that wants to be revealed is in the expression of pain and shame that we have hidden, inherited, and passed on, and that we are now called upon to dignify.

10

Sacred Agreements with Rage

As our rage child continues to reveal herself, she has the power to run buck wild and work against us if we fail to give her proper attention. Being right too long can actually be wrong. For example, early in my healing journey, I remember a particular session with my therapist. Unknowingly solid in my *Defiance* disguise, I was complaining about the insensitive white men on my job and how I hated them. How they didn't listen and how I felt ignored. How I couldn't understand why, when I pointed out to them how screwed up they were, they mistreated me even more. I was going on and on. My therapist listened with loving ears and observed with loving eyes for quite a while, then she asked matter-of-factly: *Why did you send her to the job?* Stunned, I defensively asked her what she meant. She rephrased her question to my disliking: *Why would you send a child to do a woman's job?*

My first reaction was to get pissed off at my therapist. She obviously didn't understand what I was saying. She was clearly a Black woman. Why should I have to explain what I'm talking about? *She should know.* Sitting there, I was beginning to question her true ethnicity and my judgment for selecting her as my therapist. I felt attacked. She could sense my rage in my agitation—pacing was a dead giveaway. I had a frightened look in my eyes that I get when I realize I've just been hit over the head with truth, but feel too exposed to admit it. Instead, feeling ashamed, I was determined to blame my therapist. This lasted a few more moments.

My second thought was that she *might* be on to something. After all, we had been working together for several months, and she'd been pretty right on target most other times. She kindly went on: *It sounds like such a big job for a small spirit.* We both paused a moment. She then added insult to injury: *I bet she can't even see over the steering wheel when she drives, and she could probably fit into your briefcase. Her clothes are the wrong size and she trips in those big shoes of yours. She sounds ill-equipped for the job. So why do you send her to work?*

Reality slapped me; I felt sober with pure clarity. I didn't know whether to get mad about the big shoes comment or to surrender to the simplicity of her message. Hell, it never occurred to me that my rage and I were not one and the same—that it was just a part of me, not all of me. In that moment, I had once again awakened to my rage child. I sat dumbfounded, processing the truth of her astute observation.

My therapist then asked: *What would it be like for you to make a new deal with your rage child? For example, give this part of you a warm bottle, sing her a song, and put her to bed, then send the wise woman to deal with those wolves—that part of you that is more capable of succeeding?* I thought to myself: *I could do that!* I'll never forget the instant relief and control I felt as I recognized that I was more than my rage. This was the beginning of a sacred agreement with my rage child. Such agreements are particularly helpful as we commit ourselves to living without our disguises of rage.

Disguises are like drugs and we can go through withdrawals without them. They numb us from experiencing the rage we feel toward our own helplessness and the shame we have felt from being dishonored and disrespected.

Following are exercises to help us establish sacred agreements with our rage child. Settle into your sacred space, pull out your rage journal, and enjoy openheartedly setting agreements with your rage child.

APOLOGY

This is your opportunity to explain and apologize to your rage child for imposing adult responsibilities on her as a child spirit. Use this template as a guide when apologizing to your rage child: *I'm sorry for . . . It was my fault that . . . Please forgive me for . . . I forgive myself for . . .* Fill in the blanks and add statements that are most appropriate for you. Speak directly to the heart of your rage child. Here are a few examples:

- I'm sorry for silencing you with drugs.
- It was my fault that I let you drive when I was drunk. I'm sorry I abandoned you and put us in danger.
- Please forgive me for using you to communicate my pain to the outside world. I realize now that your voice belongs first to my ears and heart.
- Please forgive me for ignoring the many ways you have tried to be a close friend.
- I'm sorry for sending you to my job when I should have gone myself.
- Please forgive me for not knowing how to love you. I didn't understand your gifts of truth, clarity, and warmth.

APPRECIATIONS

Appreciations help us let go from the heart and move forward more kindly and humbly. Sharing appreciations are ways you can tell your rage child how grateful you are for the many ways she has contributed to your survival. Look back over your life and notice how an enraging time may have given you much growth and insight. Take your time and be specific as you recall how your rage child has helped you endure and make sense out of life. Here are some examples:

- I appreciate that you are always making a fuss when my boundaries are violated.
- I appreciate how you help me write the truth and remember what happened to me as a child.
- I appreciate how you made me ill and forced me to take a rest.
- I appreciate how you have played a leading role in my activism. Thank you for teaching me how to fight for what is right.
- I appreciate how you kept me alive by staying silent during my rape.
- I appreciate how your energy helps me paint, write poetry, and play the piano.

Capture your appreciations as often as you can recall them, and rest in knowing that your rage child has been on your side, fighting for your well-being, even while being denied by you and ill-equipped for the job. Appreciations help your rage child soften, stop crying, and stop rebelling. Our rage child has not always known what to do with our truth, but with your attention and support, she can rest.

NEW RULES

New rules affirm to your rage child that you are now the parent and she the child spirit, and that things will be both different and better. Most children need structure. They need to have clear parameters and the limits must be directly stated and reinforced. Your rules communicate how you plan to tap the truth of your rage child—to listen to her truth without harming others and yourself. Here you instruct your rage child on how to contact you and how she can best support you. Here are examples:

- From now on, you do not make the ultimate decisions in my life.
- As of this day, I am removing your privilege to drink and drive.
- When I want to talk to you and need your wisdom, I will alert you with five minutes of deep breathing and ten minutes of listening.
- When you want to alert me, you may cause me to perspire. I will get still and listen.
- Starting today, you will take a daily nap lasting from 8:00 A.M. to 5:00 P.M. while I am at work.
- When I get home from work, we can share insights and learn together.
- Sugar, alcohol, and caffeine are not good for you and will be used sparingly.

COMMITMENTS

Commitments are ways of declaring your intention to be a wise, nurturing mother to your rage child, reassuring this fierce spirit of how you plan to take care of yourself so she does not have to resort to disguises. For example, you may celebrate her birthday each year, or

determine specific dates and times when you attend to her and nurture your relationship more genuinely. Here are some examples of
commitments:

- From now on, you have my undivided attention every morning
  for ten minutes in our sacred space.
- I commit to talk to you every day and ask how you feel and what
  you need.
- I commit to practice living without disguises so that you are
  able to help instead of hurt my life.
- When I'm upset, I'll remember to check in with you and ask
  your opinion about the situation.

Make commitments that you feel you can keep. Start with one or
two commitments and increase them as you become clearer and feel
successful.

We are challenged with parenting ourselves as we have never been
parented, and loving ourselves as we have never been loved. Love
heals rage and sacred agreements are kindhearted practices for building an intimate relationship with your rage child.

After you have completed journaling these agreements, sit quietly
in gratitude for all that you have endured, for all that you have overcome, and for all that you will transform. Feel free to add to your sacred agreements as you continue to awaken to your rage child.

11

Solving Rage Riddles—
Looking *In* before Acting *Out*

Healing rage does not mean we eliminate or never feel rage. We will continue to be provoked in the world, thrown off center, and at times will need to dress up in our disguises. Yet each time we react in a knee-jerk fashion to rage instead of responding thoughtfully, we betray ourselves. We give our rage child away, will her truth over to some other power. We deplete ourselves of vital energy before it has fed us, and we feel ashamed because we are vulnerable—overexposed and under-protected.

When we are triggered by the aggression or ignorance of others, an accumulation of anger, shame, and fear can brim over. What we do next is not only crucial but also within our control. Harriet Lerner, author of *The Dance of Anger,* shares: *Anger is a tool for change when it changes us to become more an expert on the self and less of an expert on others.*

To respond outwardly in a responsible way requires that we understand our inner-rage experiences. The following exercises teach us how to examine our thoughts to better understand our rage experiences;

we learn to speak truthfully and mindfully, without harming others or ourselves, and we learn to listen, trust ourselves, and take action on our own behalf.

The benefits of these practices will not be immediately available to us in the heat of a crisis. These practices assume that we will take time to look within ourselves before acting out—scrutinize our rage triggers prior to a crisis and master a more healthy response. Understanding rage requires patience. When we maintain a consistent practice, spend quality time in our sacred space, and keep our rage journal handy, rage ceases to be a problem we overidentify with and overreact to.

TRUTH-TELLING

One of my meditation instructors, Michele Benzamin-Miki, tells the story of a poor Tibetan woman running through the streets screaming, *Thief! Thief!* Everyone in the village runs to her aid intent on protecting her, only to discover she is calling attention to herself—*she* is the thief. I love this story because it invites us to imagine exposing those aspects of ourselves that we disown yet so quickly judge in others. We may not feel much affection, in this case, for a thief, but what we fear even more is being exposed as one—to roam the streets of our hearts proclaiming, *Thief! Thief!* Yet such truth has an immediate effect on our ability to let go and rest within our body and mind.

Truth-telling is best practiced when you have intense feelings of agitation, guilt, frustration, fear, or fury, and you want to understand more deeply, defuse, and own what you are experiencing. Don't try to be logical or reasonable, just be honest. Acknowledge your first thoughts or top feelings.

Sit quietly in your sacred space and listen without judgment or shame. When you have settled your body and mind with *Being Now*, explore the following questions:

Looking In before Acting Out

• What old pain or story does this feeling evoke?
• What does my rage child want me to learn from this situation?
• Does this situation energize or deplete me?
• What might I gain if I let go of my point of view?
• Is this disturbance a priority or a diversion?
• In what ways am I contributing to my own suffering?
• How can I give myself what I need right now?
• What action can I visualize that would build connection and not cause harm?
• Before you take action, consider:
  ◦ What can I do that would foster goodwill and well-being?
  ◦ What can I do that will be respectful?
  ◦ What can I do that will minimize pain and suffering in others?
  ◦ What can I do that will enhance my relationships?
  ◦ What can I do that will acknowledge my contribution to the problem?
  ◦ What can I do that will make my ancestors proud?
  ◦ What can I do that will support my healing intentions?

Ask any other questions you may have that will help you to understand the truth you are feeling. When you feel satisfied with this inquiry, spend a few moments journaling. The point of this exercise is to look within to acknowledge and understand your true experience. We heal by becoming self-aware. Truth-telling is a humbling and humanizing exercise that gifts us with inner comfort and self-respect.

OBSERVATIONS AND INTERPRETATIONS

One way of solving rage riddles is to separate observations from interpretations. An observation is neutral, like a video camera capturing what is seen and heard through its lens. An interpretation poses meaning and influences our feelings about what is being observed. For example:

Observation	Interpretation
She is speaking loudly and frowning.	She is angry with me.
The leadership team is all white.	The leadership team is racist.
He is a Harvard graduate.	He thinks he is better than everyone.

Interpretations often arise from the soil of our rage disguises and represent narrow ways of understanding what is taking place. Many of us fast-forward through our observations as mindlessly as we might operate the remote control of a TV. This impulse is almost reflexive, and common. Slowing down our thinking to observe more objectively causes us to feel more, and feeling more can make us uncomfortable. We feel safer with our hasty interpretations, convincing ourselves that they are the whole truth. Often our interpretations are accurate and valid, but when we suspend them, we open ourselves to the experience of not knowing, or better yet, knowing more. In this spaciousness, we may consider many possible interpretations, including none at all. Often our curiosity will arise in the absence of interpretations, giving us an opportunity to explore new meaning.

Observation	Interpretation	Exploration
She is speaking loudly and frowning.	She is angry with me.	I wonder what she's feeling. I wonder what she needs.
The leadership team is all white.	The leadership team is racist.	Are they aware of the impact of an absence of diversity? Are they seeking more diversity?
He is a Harvard graduate.	He thinks he is better than everyone.	I don't know much about him. I wonder if he liked attending Harvard.

Practice separating your observations from interpretations throughout the day and especially following the truth-telling exercise. Your interpretations may often be accurate, but it is good practice to examine them to ensure that your rage child is not distorting your view. Hers is not the whole truth, nor should her emotional trigger be your first priority. When our interpretations become our only truth, they rob us of energy that would otherwise go toward us connecting more genuinely with others and ourselves.

PAIN AND SUFFERING

Behind rage is pain, not just the stories we tell ourselves. We have feelings about what is occurring, and we use our interpretations to short-circuit or separate from what we are feeling. In other words, we use interpretations not to feel. When this occurs we suffer. Distinguishing between our pain and our suffering provides us with the option to suffer less.

For example, we may accidentally cut our finger while chopping vegetables in the kitchen. Blood is running all over our evening meal. These are clear observations, and we are in pain. However, we suffer when our mind takes over and creates a larger story, or interpretation: *Oh my God, I'm going to bleed to death. I knew this would happen. I hate that damn knife. This will leave a scar. I'm so stupid. How will I play the piano? Why didn't XYZ chop these vegetables? This shit always happens to me*, etc. The interpretations that we lay on top of our original pain cause us to suffer and separate from the experiences we are having in that moment. In our attempt to avoid pain, we create more of it, and we are not taking care of the immediate need. In the above example, the reality is that we have cut ourselves, we are hurting, and we need to take care of ourselves. Dealing with our pain is what is now, and what needs our attention. The rest of the dread is suffering and optional. Similarly, if you saw a child struck by a hit-and-run driver, your impulse would be to comfort the child, not run after the car. In the same way, when we are triggered, we are in pain, and our pain needs our comforting attention. In these moments, we want to stay with our pain and begin to explore what we may need. Let's apply this idea to our earlier examples:

Observation	Pain	Suffering (an interpretation we apply to avoid pain)	Exploration
I cut my finger.	I'm hurting.	I knew this would happen.	Why am I beating myself up? I'm already hurting!
She is speaking loudly and frowning.	I'm frightened.	She is angry with me.	Why am I afraid of people who speak loudly and frown?
The leadership team is all white.	I feel excluded.	The leadership team is racist.	Why is inclusion by white people important to me?
He is a Harvard graduate.	I feel inadequate.	He thinks he is better than everyone.	What is it about Harvard [or higher education] that makes me feel inadequate?

Begin to notice when you are suffering more than you need to. Drop the suffering and comfort the pain. It is our response to what life offers that causes us suffering—not what life offers.

PROJECTIONS AND PERCEPT LANGUAGE

Upon closer inspection of our truth, we ultimately find that what enrages us most is recognizing ourselves in others—often a shocking discovery. For example, let's say our Harvard graduate *does* think he is better than everyone. Why is this important to *you*? Why do you suppose this matter catches *your* attention? The fact that it catches your attention is saying something about you!

This is a psychological concept known as *projecting*, meaning that when you interpret someone as being angry, what you are experiencing is the *angry part of you* reflected in that person. You zoom in on it because it is your projection—an unconscious, feared, or denied part of your experience. Of course, this is not always the case. Sometimes people are wicked, hateful, and violent. However, more often, we see what we fear and deny most, and we see what we expect to see.

We project when we can't tolerate our full selves. We are projecting when we can judge others without recognizing that we, too, behave or have behaved in similar ways, albeit under different circumstances. Individuals, families, communities, and even nations make projections. It is a common, fear-based practice that perpetuates separation and suffering.

Percept Language

Percept is a Jungian-based technique that allows us to experiment with the notion that all that is occurring in any given situation is a projection of our own experience. I was first introduced to this tool while attending a self-differentiation workshop offered by Joyce and John Weir, an elderly couple who had worked together for more than thirty years in the group dynamics community.

The *Percept* technique is simple. It presumes that whatever catches your attention in life is a *part of you*. This technique has been highly useful in understanding rage. Plainly stated, it invites you to add the words *part of me* to every person, character, and object in situations of high distress. Adding the words *part of me* helps you pause, expand your assumptions, and reclaim your projections. You claim each aspect of your own experience and further examine the nature of each aspect independently.

Let's apply the *Percept* technique to an earlier example. Basically, you witness what is occurring (*Observation* and *Interpretation*) and apply the *Percept* language *part of me* to the end of your interpretation, after which you look inward (*Exploration*) to discover the messages your rage child is offering you.

Observation	Interpretation	Percept	Exploration
She is speaking loudly and frowning.	She is angry at me.	She is an angry *part of me*.	What part of me is angry and needs my attention?

Here, we are applying *Percept* to the interpretation of *angry*. It can as easily be applied to the observations of *loudly* and *frowning*—loud *part of me*, and frowning *part of me*. We would explore these parts of ourselves by asking: *In what ways am I afraid of living loudly? What am I frowning on in my life these days?* *Percept* offers us an opportunity to look within ourselves and explore the gifts that our present circumstances are invoking. Let's explore another earlier example:

Observation	Interpretation	Percept	Exploration
The leadership team is all white.	The leadership team is racist.	The leader *part of me* is a racist *part of me*.	How am I leading in my life? In what ways am I racist?

Percept application does not mean to suggest that what we observe and interpret outside ourselves is all about us and what we project. Life is more complex and clearly there are times when people and situations are hurtful, and their behaviors are not directly related to our personal projections. However, when what we see and feel pierces our hearts and grabs hold of our attention consistently, our rage child is shouting, *Thief! Thief!* and inviting us to reclaim and comfort her.

Percept and Dream Interpretations

The *Percept* technique is also an insightful tool for dream interpretation. Our dreams are rich with rage riddles—messages embedded in the dreams that are ripe for decoding. *Percept* presumes that every character or object in our dreams is a *part of you*. For example, if your mother appears in your dream, the dream is not necessarily about your mother but may be more about the mother *part of you*. You may ask yourself: *What feelings or attributes do I most associate with my mother?* Your response to this question would be what is referenced as a *part of you* in your dream.

The *Percept* application to dreams is simple:

A. Before going to bed, invite your dreams to reveal themselves to you. Commit to wake up long enough to write down your dreams. Have your rage journal and pen near your bedside.

B. Write your dreams in the present tense—as if they are occurring right before you. If you find you cannot recall the entire dream, that's not a problem. Just write any feelings, images, or thoughts that you are having in that moment.

   • Note: Go back to sleep if you like. You can do the next steps later.

C. Read through the dream and add *part of me* to the end of key people, places, things, actions, and feelings.

D. Reread your dreams and explore their many meanings.

Marva, disrobing the *Depression* disguise of rage, and grieving abandonment by her father and physical abuse by her mother, wrote the following dream during a Celebration of Rage™ retreat:

> A man is captured by the police, hit on the head, and knocked out. They drag him out. Others watch and call the guy a fool for breaking the rule. I'm thinking: Why fight them. You can't win! You are outnumbered.

When Marva applies the *Percept* technique, the dream reads as follows:

A **man** part of me is a **captured** part of me by the **police** part of me, **hit** part of me on the **head** part of me, and **knocked** part of me **out** part of me. The **man** part of me is a **drag** part of me **out** part of me. **Other** parts of me **watch** part of me and **call** part of me a **fool** part of me for **breaking** part of me the **rules** part of me. The **thinking** part of me **asks** parts of me: **Why fight** parts of me. The **outnumbered** parts of me are **always wins** part of me.

After applying the *Percept* technique, Marva solves her riddle of rage by discovering how she has internalized her abuse from childhood and can now transform it. Here is how the *Percept Language* helped in her dream interpretation:

I'm still angry at my father [male, captured] for abandoning me so I abandon myself [knocked out, dragged out] and I abuse myself [hit on head] just as my mother abused me. I witness my abuse [others watch] and don't stop it, and I blame myself [fool] for thinking that I could free myself [breaking the rules]. I feel helpless and hopeless in defending myself [why fight, you can't win, you are outnumbered]. I'm capable of watching/witnessing myself [watch, thinking and asks] therefore I am capable of taking charge and changing my view of self-protection [male, police].

This dream can undoubtedly be interpreted in any number of ways, but what is most important is Marva's interpretation. Marva felt she had a better understanding of her anger and self-abuse, how her past still lived in the present, and that she is capable of redefining how she protects herself.

The *Percept* technique provides simple and often profound insights and can be equally applied to journal entries as well as to other observations and interpretations in your life.

Dreams help us become more aware of our wholeness and of the world we behold. They can show us where we are stuck and what wants to be freed. Once we understand our dreams, we further liberate ourselves. Become acquainted with the active wisdom of rage while you sleep. Discover how your rage child delights and finds complete expression in this subconscious realm of creative freedom.

12

Meditations with Rage

Some people say watch your tongue. No, watch your mind because the tongue does not wag itself!

Bhante Henepola Gunaratana

ABOUT MEDITATION

There is no greater gift to our rage child than our willingness to be present with her, and we do this most effectively through meditation. Meditation soothes the hot coals of inner rage and helps us suffer *less*. Through meditation, we teach the mind to ride the energies of rage without battle so that we become aware of what we deeply know and need to heal. When we meditate, we are training the mind to stop feeding a pain pattern—our disguises of rage. We are learning how to stay present, and growing in our awareness that the present moment is worth coming back to and living fully.

Meditation is not recommended here as a way to eradicate our rage, but as a way to become fully present to its energies. Our rage disguises are held in place by a desperate attempt to escape from the intolerable past, and in so doing, we have distanced ourselves from the truth and vitality that is available to us in the present moment.

Meditation is not a quick fix. It asks us to slow down so that we can experience ourselves *lovingly*. There are many benefits derived from a consistent meditation practice. Meditation opens us to levels of consciousness that lie deeper than our intellect. Our disguises fade and our aggression diminishes. Our mind becomes tranquil and more manageable, and we act more wisely toward others and ourselves. Not only does meditation decrease fear and worry, it also reduces our heart rate, blood pressure, respiratory rate, oxygen consumption, perspiration, and muscle tension, and improves our immune system and neurotransmitter function. All this, and it's free! Through meditation, we cultivate inner peace.

In many ways, meditation may seem counterintuitive to healing rage, but it is indeed an act of tremendous self-compassion and respect. While many traditional religions and spiritual paths offer some form of contemplation such as prayer, chants, or song, maintaining a consistent meditation practice is a wholesome and practical way to heal rage.

The following meditations are inspired from the Vipassana Buddhist tradition and are intended to enhance your daily *Stillness Practice* introduced in an earlier chapter. *Vipassana* is a Pali word meaning *insight*, and its goal is liberation through awareness. In Vipassana meditation, compassionate attention is directed to an examination of our inner way of being. This compassionate attention, with practice, sooths the inner heat of rage, and we find ourselves less reactive to what life offers.

GETTING STARTED

It is useful to meditate at the same time and place each day. Start with a short amount of time and gradually increase the time. Hilda Ryumon Baldoquin, a Soto Zen meditation master, suggests to beginners the 5/5/5 Rule: Meditate for five minutes a day, five days a week, for five weeks in a row. Practicing consistently tells the mind that you mean business and reassures your rage child that there is safe space for her development.

Concentration will develop over time. In the early stages of your daily practice, you may experience a range of emotions that distract your concentration. For example, you may become fretful, annoyed, sluggish, sleepy, or numb when you sit still. Don't be alarmed and don't give up. Make sure you are seated comfortably in a chair or on a cushion, as if your flesh were loosely hanging on a straight but relaxed spine.

Your meditation will be affected by what you eat and drink. Avoid meditating on a full stomach. Also, sugar, alcohol, and excessive carbohydrates have an effect on concentration and physical comfort. Become aware of how these substances affect you and use this awareness to make appropriate choices.

Begin and end your meditations with a simple ritual. For example, I begin each meditation by lighting a candle while stating an intention. I then pay respect to my teachers and ancestors by calling out their names. I end with a gratitude prayer dedicating the merit of my good intentions to all sentient beings throughout the world. I then blow out my candle and journal what I am feeling and thinking. That's it! Create a simple yet meaningful meditation ritual that frames your practice. Eventually, such a practice is internalized and carried throughout your day with each breath.

BREATH AWARENESS

Breath gives life to the body. Breathing is the first thing we do when we are born and the last thing we do at death, yet we are seldom conscious of breathing and commonly underutilize our breath. For example, we may inhale and hold our breath too long, causing tension to build up in the body. Or we exhale for too long and experience anxiety, then gasp for our next breath. Or our breathing is shallow, as soft as a whisper, or too fast, like a panting dog. When someone yells at us, we may hold our breath to lessen the intensity of their hurtful words. Too often, and without our awareness, we use our breath to not feel.

Conversely, as we begin to notice our breath, we can notice when we hold on and when we let go. Most profoundly, becoming more mindful of breathing makes our body more alive and reliable, a place to rest and gain tremendous insight. Most practically, our breath is the primary and most affordable tool we have for purifying and reuniting our body, mind, and emotions. Breath keeps open the emotional space that our rage child requires to liberate itself.

Breath Awareness is a useful way to begin and end each day. It offers an immediate way to attune our mind to our body, and to decompress from intense moments. It is a helpful exercise anytime we want to settle ourselves, especially when we feel overwhelmed, frightened, or angry.

To begin this meditation, sit quietly in your sacred space and begin to breathe naturally. You don't need to change your breathing, just become softly aware of it. Notice the sensations of air coming in and going out at the tip of your nostrils. If you do not feel this sensation, notice your chest area expand and contract. Begin to float on the waves of your breath with each inhalation, noticing how and where the body swells. With each exhalation, allow yourself to surrender, let go, and rest in the stillness that presents itself briefly just before your next inhalation. Notice with soft attention where your breath begins and ends in your body—how and where breath touches you. Know that just as there is space between each inhalation and exhalation, there is space in your body between the organs, bones, and joints. Mentally visualize yourself breathing in and out of these spaces, opening to a full breath.

Continue to breathe in and out, concentrating on each phase of your breath—inhaling, floating, exhaling, surrendering, and resting. As you breathe—*in and out, in and out*—the soft rhythm of your breath begins to sing a soothing lullaby to your rage child. As you rest in your body, you simultaneously give your rage child more space to feel relaxed, safe, and at home. The great news about *Breath Awareness* is that it does not require you to go anywhere. It is immediate, constant, and free. It is your private inner*tame*ment. Sit. Breathe. Relax. Notice. Enjoy.

MIND AWARENESS

It's ok to have all these thoughts, just don't believe them!

HILDA RYUMON BALDOQUIN, Soto Zen Priest

The mind's job is to be busy with thought—24/7. The problem is that we often confuse the activities of the mind with the whole truth, rather than an ever-changing moment. A single wave of emotion can feel like the vast ocean at any given time, yet it is still only a wave, to be followed by another wave and another. Emotions are fed by thoughts that believe they are the only reality, but they are simply events of the mind that predictably come and go. What we feel and think changes constantly.

My beloved teacher, Jack Kornfield, tells of being taught to mentally bow to each of his thoughts and emotions as they arise during meditation. This simple and gracious act is a noble way to acknowledge our experiences without becoming entangled or attached to them. As we learn to compassionately witness the activity of the mind, we discover that we can be informed, even entertained, by our thoughts and feelings without the urgency to believe them or act on them.

Mind Awareness meditation is useful at any time you want to be more present with yourself, and especially when you are feeling overwhelmed, anxious, confused, hurt, frightened, or angry. Allow about fifteen minutes. Begin with *Breath Awareness*. Once you have settled yourself, begin to notice what is occurring.

Don't be alarmed if you experience a bombardment of thoughts and feelings. Nothing is wrong! The mind is doing its job. What's important to consider, however, is that the mind's job is not your life! This meditation helps with that distinction. Also, don't try to stop your mind from doing what it is doing. Rather, begin to shift your awareness from *being* the experience that is occurring to *witnessing* it. This subtle shift can be a profoundly liberating experience.

If it feels right, you may want to silently name the thoughts and feelings as they arise—*thinking, analyzing, hate, planning, afraid, happy, sad, worried, angry, bored, judgment, sleepy,* and others. Name your experiences as you are having them with soft awareness—without attachment, judgment, criticism, or stories. Simply return to your breath after each observation.

Mind Awareness meditation is basically about noticing thoughts and feelings, naming them, and returning to the breath. If you become impatient, and start to beat yourself up, acknowledge your experience: *Impatience . . . Beating myself up . . .* then return to the breath. This is the *mindful* practice—returning to the breath *again and again and again.*

Sometimes our experiences will be liberating, other times frightening, and every experience you can imagine in between. The good news is that our experiences are seldom the same, nor do they last forever. Instead, we experience a constant stream of emotion, thought, and sensation, and this meditation helps us notice and *bow* to them.

Keep in mind that we are not attempting to stop the mind from doing what it does; we simply want to bring kind awareness to it. We are training the mind to bear witness to its experience.

After meditating on *Mind Awareness,* spend some time writing in your rage journal. Consider these questions without judging your experience:

- What thought or emotion predominated my meditation practice?
- Was my primary experience pleasant, unpleasant, or neutral?

• What did my mind attach itself to—a point of view, fantasy, blame, hatred, worry, or nothing at all?

The beauty of the *Mind Awareness* practice is that we cultivate self-acceptance and compassion, and discover that we have the power to witness our experiences without being confused or controlled by them.

BODY AWARENESS

We are more than intelligent minds, we are intelligent bodies, as well. Because we often suffer from a split of body and mind, we are not aware of the subtle interactions of our intelligence. Instead, we over-identify with body or mind in any given circumstance.

For example, when I ask Brenda, *How are you doing?* her immediate response is, *I'm tired and angry with the kids.* I then ask Brenda, *How is your body doing?* To this she replies, *I'd have to think about that.* Therein lies the trap—we too often feel with our mind and not our body. We have raging thoughts that we are not aware of experiencing in our body, or we have intense sensations that we can't explain. Similarly, Charlotte shares vivid details of being raped at the age of twelve. When asked what she is experiencing in her body, she replies, *Nothing.* Like Charlotte, many of us can communicate our experiences while being cut off from feeling them.

While our rage disguises live mostly in our minds, the body is where our rage wisdom lives, and where the truth of the moment lives. To experience our thoughts and feelings, we need to become still, breathe, and allow the sensations to surface.

In *Body Awareness* meditation, we open to a reunion of body and mind by exploring the sensations of our thoughts and feelings. There is a difference between a feeling and a sensation. Feelings are short-cuts, often expressed in thoughts and words: sadness, joy, disappointment, happiness, rage, etc. When we are enraged, our feelings become piercing, and generally there is an object—person, place, or thing outside of ourselves—that is the focus and cause of our suffering. Sensations are more direct experiences from the body: heavy chest, throbbing eyes, stiff lower back, tightness in the back of the head, clammy hands, tight skin, heat, cold, itchy leg, gurgling in the stomach, or sleepy foot. Sensations communicate the raw realness of the moment, and are a more reliable truth than our thoughts and feelings. In *Body Awareness*, we explore beyond our feelings to an awareness of how our feelings are being experienced in the body.

In *Body Awareness* meditation, we practice shifting our attention from the object of agitation—*the other*—to exploring how our feelings are being experienced in the body. This exercise is profoundly useful any time you feel enraged. The beauty of this exercise is discovering that when we are paying *kind* attention to rage, it often ceases to become a problem.

Allow about twenty minutes. Relax into your sacred space. Begin with *Breath Awareness* and acknowledge to yourself that you are safe. Keep in mind that throughout this exercise your breath is your anchor, and you can return to it any time you need to calm yourself.

When you are ready, invite the object of your agitation to reveal itself in full bloom in your mind's eye. See yourself in the righteousness of your frustration and allow this upset to get as large and as intense as it needs to. Breathe to stay present, and take your time. Allow this experience for a while. When you are ready, see yourself turning away from the object of frustration and focusing your attention on your sensations—the way your body is experiencing frustration.

Softly begin to notice your experience in terms of sensations—what is occuring within your body in the absence of thoughts or feelings. For example, you may find yourself thinking: *I'm sad, I'm angry?* If so, direct your attention to the sensations you are experiencing in your body that may be feeding this thinking: *What sensations inform me that I am sad and angry?* Continue this exploration—breathing and bearing kind witness as each sensation arises and passes away.

Take your time and give your sensations your full attention. As you are allowing your sensations to be fully explored, consider sending compassion and kindness to yourself by repeating these phrases:

- *May I be free from suffering and the cause of suffering.*
- *May I experience what life offers with kindness.*
- *May I be free from harming myself and others.*
- *May I be happy loving myself right here, right now.*

Notice how these statements affect your experience—what sensations arise. Continue riding the winds of your breath, allowing your body to be present with you in its unique way. When you are done, gently end your meditation and journal your experience.

Body Awareness meditation helps you discover how your body tells a deeper truth than the mind and its memories. With practice, we heal our mind/body split, gain more access to our rage wisdom, and reacquaint ourselves with resting in our bodies.

Meditation is an invaluable aid to healing rage. When we maintain a consistent meditation practice, we strengthen internal wiring that allows us to carry our full life force peacefully. We learn to rest in our own skin and comprehend all that we behold.

When you become uncomfortable or frightened, remember that difficult emotions are your most profound teachers. The more we can witness our experiences without judgment, the less suffering we experience in our lives. We eventually learn to rest in the ebb and flow of the present moment, experiencing it as pure, often pleasant, and ever-changing. We begin to trust that what feels frightening and intolerable does not last forever.

Through our meditations with rage, we embrace an inner peace that affirms that change is simply our nature—neither good nor bad.

We soften our hold on the faulty assumption that one experience, joy, is always better than another, rage. We discover how to rest in the seasons of rage. We accept gracefully that everything changes all the time within us, within others, and within the world.

We become sensitive to our actual experience of living, and to how it feels to be a seasonal human being. We can feel more love toward others because we understand them, and we understand others because we understand ourselves. The greater this compassion, the more inner peace is possible.

13

Uprooting Your
Rage Inheritance

We are children of a common womb.
LUISAH TEISH, author of *Carnival of the Spirit*

To uproot our rage inheritance is to turn inward to see baggage we've been hauling, open it up, and shine a light inside. And by shining a light on our rage inheritance—doing our own work of healing—we can create a new legacy.

Our rage inheritance is most often rooted in childhood traumas that were not responded to properly. Stated simply, many of us feel that our rage is rooted in a disconnect from our parents or guardians. Children need the love of their parents. Even if our parents are deceased, many of us still yearn for a closer and more genuine relationship with them. We long to be loved and cherished as their children and respected and acknowledged as powerful people in our own right. Regardless of our independence and worldly accomplishments, we can be perplexed and emotionally disabled by the continuing power of these primary relationships.

The truth is that we can never fully discover, uncover, or understand all the stories that make up our rage inheritance. Many stories may have been lost, and people who are alive may be unwilling to break their silence or shine a light on their own experiences. Yet as we open ourselves to more emotional truth, we may begin to feel the heavy burden of our rage inheritance—a burden whose contents still live in our bones and in our nervous systems, having survived untold generations.

We dwell on things because they are unfinished, and we have an unconscious loyalty to our past that we must make conscious in order to heal. To begin to be at ease within ourselves requires that we be willing to understand our parents' rage histories and rage inheritances, and how they, as humans, have grown to give and receive love. The ultimate reason we want to uproot our rage inheritance is to make an explicit agreement to put to rest what is already behind us, especially those things that trouble the mind. This exercise helps us make sense out of our lives and enables us to make choices that positively affect ourselves and future generations. Uprooting our rage inheritance has four parts.

Part 1: *Imagining*—Because the spirits of our parents and ancestors live inside our bones and in our hearts, we first turn within ourselves and visualize separate conversations with our parents, guardians, and ancestors, to imagine their lives and their rage inheritances.

Part 2: *Conversations with Parents and Elders*—We physically interview our parent or parents, if they are living, and/or the elders in our family, to learn more about their lives and rage inheritances.

Part 3: *Discerning the Gifts of Our Rage Inheritance*—We sort through the information we have gathered—the bones of our inheritance—separating the gifts from those that are to be put to rest.

Part 4: *Amending the Soil of Rage*—We alter our rage inheritance by adding the nutrients of compassion, understanding, patience, and wisdom to our healing intentions.

PART 1: IMAGINING

You begin in your sacred space envisioning yourself asking questions of your parents and ancestors, utilizing the *Rage Inheritance Questionnaire* below, and opening yourself for answers. This visualization can be insightful even if you already know the details of your parents' childhoods, but especially if you don't. You may find that your mind *knows* their histories but has never paused long enough for your heart to *feel* them.

This exercise is also useful to invite the rage wisdom of your ancestors to make itself known. For example, you might have an ancestor whose struggles with rage are similar to your own. Or you may have an ancestor you have called on in times of need. It could be someone your heart went out to because you watched helplessly as they suffered from direct experiences of rage or some other related trauma. Or it may be someone you never knew personally but wanted to know. It may not be a blood ancestor at all but rather someone you felt a kinship with.

You may have lost or never known the stories of your ancestors, yet their spirits are alive nonetheless. You can invite them in and ask them questions about their lives and their rage inheritance, and they will be inclined to answer and pleased to share their insight, for they too have suffered needlessly from family and world legacies of rage. They know the futility of your suffering from their own experiences.

This imagining exercise is a safe dress rehearsal for Part 2, should you desire to physically interview your living parents and/or elders. However, even if you choose not to perform an actual interview, clarifying your questions about your parents' lives and imagining their responses can still be deeply helpful.

To begin, review the *Rage Inheritance Questionnaire* below and select five to seven questions to explore with each of your parents and ancestors. If the questions that you feel are most important are not listed, feel free to create new ones. Consider spacing this exercise out over several

Stillness Practices. For each imagining exercise, allow at least twenty minutes. Keep your rage journal nearby to record your experiences.

Rage Inheritance Questionnaire

As a Child

1. Do you know the circumstances that surrounded your birth?
2. What is your sweetest memory as a child?
3. When did you realize you were special? How did you know?
4. Who were your role models when you were young? Why?
5. What was most important to you as a child? Why?
6. What story did your mother tell you that helped you most in life? Your father? Your caretaker?
7. Have you ever been accused of something you didn't do? What?
8. As a child, how many children did you think you would have as a grown-up? Why?
9. What was the most devastating injustice you personally experienced?
10. What physical or emotional illnesses did you struggle with as a child? Why?

Happiness

11. Why are your hobbies and special talents important to you?
12. What are the lyrics of your favorite songs? Why do you love them?
13. When was the happiest time of your life? Describe it in full detail.
14. What is your most valued personal possession?
15. Who's been your best friend? Why?
16. What do you love about yourself?
17. Who was your most significant love? Why?
18. What were the positive circumstances that surrounded my birth?

19. What did you love most about your mom? Your dad?
20. If you were a painter, what would you paint?
21. What song have you always wanted to write? To sing? To hear?
22. Who was your favorite actor, singer, activist, and role model? Why?
23. What impact has your ability to love had on your life?
24. How has my life changed you?

Disappointments

25. Who or what hurt you the most in life? Why?
26. When did your heart first start to close? Why?
27. What is your earliest experience of letting go? Of being let go of?
28. What were you looking for when you married/partnered (or chose not to)? Did you find it? Why or why not?
29. Why was it necessary to end the relationship with my mom/dad? What would have needed to happen for it to last? What did you learn from this experience?
30. What is your biggest regret/disappointment with your children?
31. How have I disappointed you?
32. What would you hate for any child to experience?
33. What is difficult to hear from your children? Why?
34. Who and what are you unable to forgive?
35. What was your biggest loss? What would you give to get it back?
36. What is your biggest regret?

Challenges

37. What is the most difficult decision you've ever made? What did you learn from it?
38. What is the most difficult decision you *still* must make?
39. How have you been labeled? What would others like to change about you?

40. What is the most significant change you've made in your life? Why'd you do it?
41. What would you hate others to know about you?
42. What is your biggest fear? What is your biggest regret?
43. What physical or emotional challenges do you face? How old are they?
44. What are you most vulnerable about? What pierces your heart?
45. What are you yearning for, wanting in your life right now? Why?
46. How have your children changed you?

Endings

47. What important message have you stressed throughout your life? Why is it important? What difference has it made?
48. Has your life turned out the way you had hoped? How so? Why not?
49. What are you most proud of? Why?
50. What would you change or do over in your life? Why?
51. How do you want to live before you die?
52. What would you like to have forgiven before you die? Who or what would you like to forgive?
53. What would be your ideal way to die?
54. How would you like to be remembered?

Gifts

55. How do you feel about how I have lived my life?
56. How have we contributed to each other's well-being?
57. What lesson do you hope I get from you before you or I die?
58. What encouragement do you have for me?
59. In what ways have you felt loved by me?
60. What gift do you hope I bring to the world?

Once you have selected the questions for which you seek answers, write them in your journal. The following format might be helpful:

Questions for My Father	Questions for My Mother	Questions for My Ancestors
1.	1.	1.
2.	2.	2.
3.	3.	3.
4.	4.	4.
5.	5.	5.
6.	6.	6.
7.	7.	7.

Keep in mind that you are performing a ritual when you investigate the spirits of your parents and ancestors. Your intentions should be pure and steeped in reverence. Your spirit can heal and your life can be enhanced immeasurably when you invite the spiritual wisdom of your parents and ancestors with a healing intention.

In your sacred space relax into the *Being Now* mantra. When you feel grounded, light a candle as you state the name of the person you are inviting to be present. Visualize that person comfortably before you. As you see the person clearly in your mind, silently state your intention. For example, if you are working with your father, you might say to yourself: *Father, I am seeking a deeper understanding of my rage and ask for your support. Can you be with me? Can you share your wisdom and truth with me?* When you feel your requests have been acknowledged, ask one of your questions. Take your time, remembering to breathe fully and stay receptive and soft all over.

Repeat this process until you have asked all of your questions. When you feel complete, journal your experiences. Include the responses to the questions you asked, but especially to those you didn't verbalize. Also record how you felt asking the questions, and include any additional questions you might want to ask later. End your visualization by thanking their spirit and other sacred spirits for being present, and blow out that particular candle.

Once you have begun this exercise, avoid debating, arguing, dismissing, or judging your experiences. Simply allow the questions themselves to deepen your experience. Listen to the responses with your entire body, not just your ears. For example, you may receive a response as a mental image, a memory, a smell or sound, a taste in your mouth, a physical sensation, or nothing at all.

Not getting a response does not mean this exercise is not working. No response *is* a response. Some answers need time to reveal themselves. Stay open to receiving insight and ask the questions again at a later time. The responses to your questions may continue to unfold outside of the *Imagining* exercise. You may get an answer to one of your questions as a thought on your way to work, or in the middle of grocery shopping. A response may arise from something someone else said, or it may occur in your dreams.

For example, during a tour of the temple of Seti I, in Abydos, Egypt, I was minding my own business when a large limestone wall about thirty feet tall by sixty feet long beckoned me. According to my guidebook, this was the "Gallery of Kings." It depicts Seti pointing out to his son Ramses the hieroglyphic names of thirty-four ancestral kings in chronological order. Seti stood tall—like the father I never had, the father I hadn't realized until this moment that I even needed or missed. Ramses stands proud next to his father, affirmed, knowing his legacy of greatness.

A lightning-bolt sensation shot through my heart, knocking me from my feet to my knees. My eyes locked onto the wall as its symbolism unfolded. The proud image of *attentive father* pierced my heart like a healing arrow, responding to a longing that was deeper than any question I could have formulated. Standing in this sacred temple, beckoned by an ancient wall of paternal lineage, I allowed myself to feel the wisdom of my ancestors supporting my healing.

Life mirrors back to us what we need and who we are. Be alert and stay open to the many ways the answers to your questions may appear in your life, and as the answers unfold, capture them like jewels in your rage journal.

You may have had a particularly challenging or abusive relationship with your parents or ancestor spirits. If so, do not feel that you need to invoke them by calling their names. Also, some ancestor spirits may want to come along uninvited, but you may not feel safe or ready to engage them honorably with your highest intentions. You can set boundaries. It is perfectly fine for you to say no to some spirits and yes to others. You are in control of your journey, and at all times you should ensure your safety.

Repeat this visualization in turn for each parent, guardian, or ancestor you choose to work with. Take your time. Allow time for rest, processing, and renewal in between each *Imagining* exercise.

PART 2: CONVERSATIONS
WITH PARENTS AND ELDERS

Once you have completed these *Imagining* visualizations, you may want to take the next step and speak directly with your parents, if they are alive and willing to participate. You can also speak to elders in your family to obtain as much information as you can to understand and uproot your rage inheritance.

It is natural for many of us to feel uncomfortable with this more intimate query. You may say to yourself: *The timing is wrong. No way. The relationship is still too hurtful. Talking with my mother/father about these tender issues is out of the question.* Or, *I'm not comfortable with asking such personal questions.* You're at a critical crossroads. You can proceed with the interviews, noting your fears but not allowing them to deny your opportunity to heal. Or, if you truly don't believe you can conduct an interview without being frightened, hurt, or provoked, delay it for a more suitable time. The *Imagining* exercise (Part 1) has already mentally provided you with an empathic experience with their lives. Should you later decide to speak to your parents, guardians, or elders directly, you can always do so. Should you choose to go forward, here are a few tips on interviewing:

1. Determine the questions you want to ask in advance. Select from the *Rage Inheritance Questionnaire* mentioned earlier, create new ones, or make revisions based on your visualization experiences. Use the following format to organize your thoughts.

Questions for My Father	Questions for My Mother	Questions for My Elders
1.	1.	1.
2.	2.	2.
3.	3.	3.
4.	4.	4.
5.	5.	5.
6.	6.	6.
7.	7.	7.

2. Make a clear request. For example, I asked my mother if she would be willing to answer a few personal questions for me about her life. She agreed and we arranged to get together. It sounds formal but it was a clear request and it was something she could do and *agreed* to do. This was better than me being indirect, then being disappointed when she became suspicious of my motives, or felt caught off guard, and resisted answering.

3. Allow enough time, at least one hour. Err on the side of more time than less.

4. Make the setting private, serene, and comfortable. Do what you can to meet in person. Avoid interruptions. Turn off cell phones, beepers, and other distractions; ask them to do the same. Consider having the conversation in conjunction with a nonthreatening companion activity such as a home-cooked meal, or a leisurely walk. Also consider being in nature. The

openness of nature can absorb the intensity of what is being shared. Sharing near a large body of water or in a spacious park or forest is also a good choice.

5. Let them do the talking. Your job is to become an empathetic anthropologist—gathering information and experiencing the information you gather from their perspectives. This means that you suspend judgment, criticism, and blame. But do ask for clarification when you don't understand what is being said.

6. Keep in mind that you are not there to change them, to be understood, to prove a point, or to like or agree with what they say. You are gathering information to expand your understanding of *their* experiences and how those experiences affected their lives, and ultimately your own.

7. Take notes or, if the person you are speaking with agrees, tape the conversation. A word of caution: Tape the conversation only if it will not interrupt or distract from a real connection. Otherwise, you can record this experience after the conversation in your rage journal.

Gathering this information can often leave you with mixed feelings. For example, you may feel disappointed by what was said or not said. Your mother or father may have avoided questions or offered answers to questions you did not ask—answers you were not prepared for. Or despite your best efforts and objective preparation, they may find themselves unexpectedly resentful, defensive, or even hostile. You may not get the chance to ask the question you most wanted to have answered. You may even be blamed or shamed for causing him or her to feel uncomfortable.

Interestingly, the most puzzling feeling of all can come when the interview turns out better than you imagined, and you now have a wealth of useful information and you don't understand why you hadn't thought of doing this sooner.

Whatever your experience, take these feelings into your *Stillness*

Practice and sit with them—observing them kindly. Let your discoveries rest within you. Allow them to simmer into wisdom. Experiencing and absorbing this information is as important as understanding it.

PART 3: DISCERNING THE GIFTS
OF OUR RAGE INHERITANCE

Discerning your rage inheritance is the act of identifying the pattern or theme that has been passed down to you to heal. You have already prepared to receive this knowledge. Your rage inheritance pattern is embedded in your rage journal (or taped) responses to the *Imagining, Rage Inheritance Questionnaire,* and *Conversations with Parents and Elders* exercises. The next task is to review your notes. When you have reviewed your notes, ponder the following questions.

- How does knowing more about your parents and ancestors affect you?
- What is noteworthy about your parents' journeys? Your elders' journeys? Your ancestors' journeys?
- What disguises of rage did or do your parents wear in their adult lives? What traumas were their disguises rooted in?
- What unresolved rage would you say your parents inherited from their parents?
- What unresolved rage would you say you inherited from your parents?
- How would you characterize your rage inheritance? What themes of rage do you have in common with your parents? Ancestors? Elders?

Once you have had a chance to consider these questions, your rage inheritance may begin to reveal itself—that which has been handed down for you to heal. Awareness of your rage inheritance often deepens your commitment to healing. Susan, unmasking *Devotion* as her disguise of rage, shares:

> My father wears Defiance and has always been verbally abusive toward my mother. He didn't want to talk about this stuff. My mother wears Devotion, and during our conversation she said: "I took it for you kids!" I also learned from Mom that she had come from three generations of women who felt forced to be silent in the face of abusive husbands. But the shameful family secret that everyone lived and feared was that my mother's great-grandmother was beaten to death by her drunken husband, who was never held accountable. While I have felt stuck in a physically abusive relationship for eight years, I had no idea how old the pain was or why it was so intense. I have lived a rage inheritance of "taking a beating" out of blind allegiance to my mother. Discovering this pattern has made healing a priority. Mom may have taken the beatings for us, but I'm stopping the beatings for us.

Rage roots are strong medicine, raw with profundity, potency, and authenticity. Take your time uprooting them. Your rage inheritance may be obvious as you read through and reflect on your journal, or you may need to rest in your *Stillness Practice* for a few days until it becomes clear. Even if you have only a slight indication of a pattern, you are beginning to unearth remnants of your generational legacy that are waiting for your wise attention.

Your rage inheritance discoveries need not be shared with your living parents or elders, for it is not directly their journey. The purpose of this uprooting exercise is to discern the *essence* of your rage inheritance—the unresolved rage of your forebearers that *you* still carry—and to begin to break patterns of generational suffering.

PART 4: AMENDING THE SOIL OF RAGE

Once we have uprooted our inheritance, we can begin to amend our rage soil by adding nutrients that will ensure full-bloom fruition of our healing intentions. This ritual invites us to clearly state our intentions to break the pain patterns of our past. Fundamentally, we want to understand and honor the spirits of our parents and ancestors enough not to repeat and pass on their suffering.

Bring to your *Rage Altar* pictures, artifacts, and mementos of each spirit you are choosing to honor on your healing journey. For example, a rock from their yard, or a special token or treasure they have given you. A piece of fabric that represents your culture could be placed on your rage altar. A glass of water, flowers, and even their favorite foods can be offered as gestures of gratitude and reverence. Have several candles handy, one for each spirit you plan to honor. I associate white candles with ancestor spirits, but you may follow your own instincts and use any color you wish. Also, make sure you have your pen and rage journal on hand.

As mentioned earlier, all items you place on your *Rage Altar* should be placed mindfully with loving intention. These acts of reverence make clear to our parents' and ancestors' spirits that we acknowledge them, and accept our responsibility to transform this legacy of pain.

Sit quietly in your sacred space for several moments with *Breath Awareness* and imagine these spirits joining you in a circle of stillness. Take your time and feel their presence. When the time is right, focus your attention on each spirit separately, light a candle as you state his or her name, and begin to write a letter to this spirit. The letter should describe your rage inheritance and express your intention to transform this pain. You may also include requests for support. Note that you do not need to write a letter to each spirit in this sacred circle. You may write a letter to one or two of them and have the others witness. Always do what makes sense to you.

Once you have completed your letter, place it on your rage altar underneath your lit candle, and sit quietly in *Breath Awareness*. If you begin to sense strongly that a spirit you are addressing does not want to support you on your healing journey, honor it by removing that spirit's letter and symbols, and blowing out its candle. You can try again at a later time if you choose. Your letters can be simple and short. Here are a few examples:

Dear Dad,

We had a difficult life together yet I know you loved me and I certainly loved you—still do. Your rage and drinking got in the way of us loving each other and I have suffered greatly from not having a kind or respectful relationship with you. Just like I know you felt hated by your father, there were many times I felt you hated me, and there are times when I show hatred toward my son, to whom I haven't talked in years. I'm doing what I can to forgive you, and to forgive myself for not being able to change you. I see now that I have continued a legacy of "broken relationships with men." With this awareness, I acknowledge the pain you endured and leave that pain with you as I heal this inheritance in my life and in our family. I bring the best of your spirit with me. My prayer is that my good deeds will help your spirit rest and help me rebuild a loving relationship with my son. I ask you to watch my growth and commitment to love. Thank you, Dad. I feel you with me, and I love you. June

Dear Grandma Della,

I'm your granddaughter. We've never met because you died when you were twenty-six from breast cancer, something I am living with. Some say you were so kind it killed you. Is this true? I don't believe kindness kills. I believe it heals. But I'm so full of rage I'm not sure what's killing me—rage or cancer. Could they be one and the same? Were you, too, enraged, Grandma Della? What about your two older sisters who also died of cancer? I invite your wisdom on my journey. With your kindness, I believe I can transcend our family's legacies of rage and cancer. Your loving granddaughter, Agnes

Hello Mom,

   I want you to know that even though I haven't always liked you, I've always loved you. I better understand your coldness and your depression since I've explored the stories of your mother's line. Seems all of them were depressed, like you, like me. I realize that I'm stuck in a cycle much older than myself. Part of it may be genetic, in our blood. Maybe I'll need to struggle with depression during my life. But I want you to know that I'm laying down a part of this: the hiding, the lying, and the meanness. That stops with me. I don't know if you can join me on this journey. But I want you to know that I will always love you. I honor your life and your struggles. While you are alive, I pray that someday we can talk truthfully together. Your daughter, Esther

As you can imagine, these letters were not simple ones to write, but articulating the rage legacy is crucial to heal. The point is that each of them has discerned a pain pattern that they inherited, maintained, and even passed on out of an unconscious loyalty to their parents and ancestors. The soil of these roots is being amended by each of them taking responsibility for transforming this legacy.

Take your time, listening deep within. Be clear about the legacy you behold. The clearer you are, the more responsible you can be. Completing your letters may take several sittings—that's all right. Healing is a journey, not a destination. When you have completed your letters, thank your spirits for joining you and for informing you of your rage inheritance. Stay mindful of your intentions and commitments to heal.

When we amend the soil of our rage inheritance, we honor our ancestors and place our rage in generational perspective. In doing so, we can begin to walk more freely in our own lives, and lift a burden from future generations.

14

Gentling—
Gestures That Ripen the Heart

I heard a story about a young American man who was angry and eager to fight for the freedom of Tibet. He asked the Dalai Lama: *I'm enraged over the injustice of Tibet. It's wrong! What can I do to help?* And the Dalai Lama replied: *Take care of your own heart first. Then come! Gentling* is the practice of comforting our own pain first, and discovering that we can fight with our hearts more readily when we realize that aggression toward others harms us, and gives rise to new generations of rage. *Gentling* includes the following practices: forgiving, gratitude, affirmations, loving kindness, and compassion.

FORGIVING

The act of *Forgiving* helps us unclog the pain of our congested hearts. Healing is not dependent on whether someone forgives or understands us. We need not look outside of ourselves to be forgiven.

Rather, forgiving is an inner peace practice in which we attend directly to the pain of our own suffering.

Forgiving does not mean we condone the behavior of others or ourselves. It means we let go of the blind assumption that we can change uncontrollable situations, and we acknowledge that we have a choice to either hold or let go of our suffering. Forgiving is for our well-being and liberation, and primarily something we do in the privacy of our own heart.

Sometimes we hurt other people unknowingly. For example, we may notice that their reactions to us have changed (withdrawal, anger, or dishonor) but we're puzzled and unclear of our contribution to their behavior. Frustrated, we may feel shut out and not know how to reengage or understand what occurred. Other times, we hurt others knowingly. Feeling justified, we deliberately inflict pain through belligerence, violence, avoidance, or humiliation. Whether we know or don't know how we have hurt or harmed someone, we hurt inside of ourselves. Forgiving ourselves for our actions helps us hurt less.

Forgiving has its own season; therefore, it should not be offered insincerely. For example, if you are feeling angry or hurt over an incident or memory, and you don't feel ready to let go of these emotions, it may not be the right time for you to forgive. But know this: *Bitterness destroys the host.* You are imprisoned by your own thoughts as long as you hold onto them, and they will eventually harm you. Spend time with your rage child—reflect, journal, meditate, get to the root of your pain, or do a rage release ritual. Take care of your own pain. When the season is right for you, you can consider a conscious decision to forgive.

The following forgiveness meditation is rooted in the Vipassana tradition, which emphasizes compassionate attention toward the self. This meditation should be first practiced in the privacy of your sacred space. Once learned, however, it is best mentally practiced as often as possible and whenever you can remember to apply it—while moving from one appointment to the next, in the heat of an argument, dressing in the morning, or just before bed at night.

Begin with *Being Now* to calm yourself. Light a candle or incense to ignite your intention to forgive and invite your spirit guides for support. When you are ready, repeat the following phrases silently to become acquainted with forgiving.

- If I have hurt or harmed anyone—knowingly or unknowingly—I ask your forgiveness.
- If anyone has hurt or harmed me—knowingly or unknowingly—I forgive them.
- For all of the ways I have hurt or harmed myself, I forgive myself.

Pause after each statement and rest within your body. Welcome the thoughts, feelings, and sensations that arise with soft compassion.

These phrases are particularly useful during your *Stillness Practice*, especially as you awaken to the pain and shame your body and mind continue to hold. Sit quietly and breathe deeply. Silently repeat these phrases as the memories and images appear on the screen of your mind or show up in the sensations of your body, but only if you can express them sincerely.

You may discover that various people appear in your mind as you say these phrases. Perhaps they appear because you want to speak directly to them. If this is the case, feel free to personalize these phrases. For example, you may include the name of a person while visualizing them softly in your mind's eye, or you may be specific about the *harm* or *hurt* you are referencing. Here are some examples from other women:

- I forgive myself for leaving you, Mom. And I forgive you for not knowing how to love me.
- I forgive myself for using cocaine and harming myself.

- I forgive you, Bill, for firing me.
- I forgive myself for losing control and exploding in my meeting today.
- I forgive myself for beating my children, Anna and Ray.
- I forgive you, James, for stealing money from me and betraying my trust.
- I forgive myself for putting my children, Janice and Edna, in danger.
- I forgive myself for having an abortion.
- I forgive you, Dad, for abandoning me.

Begin a daily forgiving practice. Start small. Don't be lofty in your statements—keep it simple and sincere. Don't be alarmed if during this exercise you are unwilling to forgive. Kindly and simply say to yourself: *I forgive myself for not being willing to forgive.* Maintain a practice of forgiveness and be patient. Eventually, you will begin to experience the comfort this meditation provides.

Forgiving meditation is for your own liberation. No one else has to be involved. You need only retreat to your sacred space and practice forgiving yourself and others, and release the weight from your heart. However, sometimes the opportunity to forgive presents itself in vivid physicality, inviting your heart to respond directly. Consider the practice of stating aloud: *I'm sorry. It was my fault. Please forgive me. What can I do to help?* Anytime you can genuinely forgive, do so quickly. It brings instant relief.

Forgiving is our nature, an instinct we naturally reclaim as we heal. When we cultivate a forgiving practice, we open wide to inner peace, and outer peace becomes its manifestation.

GRATITUDE

A friend once offered me an exercise that I thought was absurd at the time, but trying it made quite a difference. She suggested that, for the next ten days, I write down ten things that I felt great about doing or seeing each day. For the first three days, I found it difficult to write even three things that I felt good about doing or seeing. By the eighth day, I had more than ten things on my list and it felt wonderful to be on the lookout for them throughout my day. When we pause a moment and notice the miracles that surround us, there is much to be grateful for and celebrate.

Every moment is a divine original, yet our lives are drenched in negativity and worry. If you were to bring sensual awareness to each moment—awareness of contact, taste, smell, sight, and sound—you would burst in aliveness, vitality, and joy, and explode in gratitude. The idea is to practice noticing the shades, gradations, and fine distinctions of your daily life. It's about being on the lookout for simple beauty and pausing to enjoy it. Wild Women Enterprises (www.wildwomen-ent.com) shares this perspective on gratitude:

- If you woke up this morning with more health than illness . . . you are more blessed than the million who will not survive this week.
- If you have never experienced the danger of battle, the loneliness of imprisonment, the agony of torture, or the pangs of starvation . . . you are ahead of 500 million people in the world.
- If you have food in the refrigerator, clothes on your back, a roof overhead, and a place to sleep . . . you are richer than 75 percent of this world.
- If you have money in the bank, in your wallet, and spare change in a dish someplace . . . you are among the top 8 percent of the world's wealthy.
- If you can read this message, you are luckier than the more than two billion people in the world who cannot read at all.

Each day, as often as you can, be grateful! Be grateful for small things and large things, beautiful things and ugly things, good things and bad things, many things and no things. Notice the miracles in your life and celebrate them, then offer your peaceful feelings to all sentient beings throughout the world. Make gratitude a twenty-four-hour practice. It lifts the spirit and ripens the heart, and it costs you nothing other than your kind attention.

AFFIRMATIONS

The mind can be tricky. Pleasant and unpleasant feelings rarely show up at the same place and time. When we are full of unpleasant thoughts—fearful, ashamed, enraged, doubtful, numb, or alone, we can balance our mind with more affirming thoughts—kindness, happiness, harmony, patience, and peace. Affirmations are antidotes to rage disguises, and help us learn that we can choose to uplift ourselves and alter our own inner experiences.

Consider the disguises of rage you wear and consult the following list of affirmations. Feel free to use any of the affirmations listed, or to create ones that affirm your specific qualities. Begin in your *Stillness Practice* with *Being Now*, allowing each breath to open your heart and soften your body and mind. State your selected affirmations slowly, and if necessary repeatedly, allowing each thought to ring true throughout your body. You may want to visualize yourself embodying these affirmations. Enjoy this exercise.

Dominance Affirmations
- I trust life.
- I flow easily with change.
- I am a part of a universal family of love.
- There is always a better way for me to experience life.
- It is safe to let go.
- I trust that the right actions are occurring in my life.
- I declare peace and harmony in my life.
- It is safe to see and experience new ideas.
- I am both powerful and desirable.

- I forgive easily and often.
- I let go of criticism effortlessly.
- I trust in the divine order of life.
- Life supports me.
- I have wonderful experiences with ease and joy.
- My good is everywhere.

Defiance Affirmations

- I am safe and free to love.
- I relax and let life flow naturally.
- I know that life supports me.
- I am free of all frustration.
- I trust that others will do what is right.
- I am kind and gentle with myself and others.
- I forgive others with ease.
- I see through eyes of love.
- I choose thoughts that make me feel good.
- I generously give and receive tenderness.
- I speak with kindness and love.
- I peacefully rest in my mind.
- I create my own experiences.
- I take time to see all sides of an issue.
- There is enough for everyone.

Distraction Affirmations

- I love my body.
- I am at peace with who I am and where I am.
- I enjoy this moment completely.
- I create only peace and harmony in my life.
- I have all that I need.
- This moment is fully satisfying.
- I only take what is offered or what is needed.
- I am deeply centered in my life.
- I am good enough.

- I love and approve of myself.
- I only attract goodness into my life.
- I easily rest in my body.
- I am healthy and happy.
- I am on a sacred journey and there is plenty of time.
- I am at ease with calm thoughts.

Devotion Affirmations
- I am worthwhile.
- I forgive myself.
- I love myself.
- Letting go is easy.
- Saying no feels good.
- I am noticed and appreciated in positive ways.
- I am at peace with all of my emotions.
- I see my own beauty and brilliance.
- I am willing to see and feel my life.
- I am safe.
- I love and approve of myself.
- Self-care is my priority.
- I am free to ask for what I want and receive it.
- I am a worthy priority.
- It is my birthright to have my needs met.

Dependence Affirmations
- I am a powerful woman.
- I am worthwhile.
- I am a success.
- I take charge of my life.
- I am free.
- I have everything I need.
- I live true to my spirit.
- I am safe and secure within myself.
- All that I need I can provide for myself.

- I can go beyond my parents' limitations.
- I have the strength and skill to handle whatever comes my way.
- I am the creative force in my life.
- I know that life supports me.
- I am perfect just as I am.
- I take care of myself.

Depression Affirmations

- It is safe to exist, to be alive.
- I am a beautiful creation.
- My life is sweet.
- My life is a joy.
- I love and cherish myself.
- I forgive myself.
- I create a life filled with rewards.
- Life loves me and I love life.
- I am filled with vibrant energy and joy.
- I create a life I love to live.
- I know that life supports me.
- I enjoy my body.
- My past strengthens me.
- It is safe for me to express my emotions.
- I trust in love and love is all around me.

KINDNESS

As we learn to make room for our overwhelming and shameful experiences, kindness plays a comforting role. Kindness and rage experiences do not generally live in the same moment, and they have an opposite effect on our mind and body. Rage can be hard and restricting, whereas kindness is soft and expanding. Both experiences have their reasons and seasons, yet our rage disguises have conditioned us away from feeling and being kind. Many of us need to relearn how to give and receive kindness and how to be kind to ourselves. Practicing kindness supports our intention to heal, and gives us courage to love our rage.

Loving Kindness, known as *Metta* in the Vipassana tradition, is the active practice of sending love and kindness to ourselves and others. *Loving Kindness* meditation does not fight our rage but embraces the heat of rage lovingly and leaves us softer, more able to rest in our wise bodies. This practice is simple and it does not require us to speak directly to anyone. It is done in silence and can be easily practiced throughout the day whenever we think about it. Traditionally, there are four phrases:

- May we be free from danger.
- May we have mental happiness.
- May we have physical happiness.
- May we have ease of well-being.

Keep in mind that these phrases are not questions—they are offerings that we direct to four audiences: ourselves, our loved ones, all conscious beings, and finally to those who have harmed us and who cause suffering in the world. When we affirm these phrases with feeling and loving intention, we are gifting kindness to ourselves and to the world.

Following is a four-step application of the *Loving Kindness* practice. Read through these instructions, then apply them from your heart. Allow about fifteen minutes for the meditation. Begin in your sacred space. Light a candle and state your intention to give and receive *Loving Kindness—Metta*. Invite your rage child and sacred spirits to join you. Begin with *Breath Awareness* followed by *Affirmations* to ground and rest in your body. When you are ready, slowly and silently apply each of the following steps.

Step 1:
We begin by first sending *Loving Kindness* to ourselves, which is often the most alien, the most difficult, and the most needed. In your

mind's eye, imagine yourself seated comfortably with your rage child lovingly cradled in your arms. Repeat these phrases or others like them slowly with your well-being in mind, and until you feel the words resting softly in your body:

- May I be well, happy, and peaceful.
- May no harm come to me.
- May I be kind, understanding, and courageous in meeting the difficulties life offers.
- May my actions in the world be motivated by kindness.
- May I be free from suffering.

Step 2:

Invite the faces of dear ones to appear—those closest to you, i.e., parents, teachers, ancestors, friends, and family members. As they appear on the screen of your mind, acknowledge their faces and their spirits in your heart. Repeat these phrases with their well-being in mind:

- May you be well, happy, and peaceful.
- May no harm come to you.
- May you be kind, understanding, and courageous in meeting the difficulties life offers.
- May your actions in the world be motivated by kindness.
- May you be free from suffering.

Step 3:

Next, imagine the billions of people and all conscious beings throughout the world. Consider the people you pass on the streets, the teller at the bank, the new boss or colleague, the ants crossing your path, the fly driving you nuts, communities and nations of poverty, the ignorant, the wealthy, all sentient beings. They, like you, need your *Loving Kindness—Metta*, compassion, and gestures that ripen the heart. Repeat the phrases above slowly and sincerely with their well-being in mind.

Step 4:

Finally, imagine those who have caused harm and suffering to you and in the world. Unfriendly people and those full of pain, greed, or hatred. Those who have innocently or willfully harmed or misunderstood you, others, communities, nations, the earth, and the world at large. Include those you feel have not been in their right mind. Yes, these individuals and institutions also need your kindness. Again, repeat the above phrases slowly with their well-being in mind.

COMPASSION

There are times during our meditations when we will feel our suffering and the suffering of others so deeply that it seems unbearable. Our tendency may be to run away from our experiences by becoming lost in thoughts, or we may overidentify with our suffering by wearing ourselves down with guilt, shame, or hopelessness. We may even terminate our meditation practice prematurely and busy ourselves with something more immediate and pleasant—shopping, eating, surfing the Internet, and even arguing are more preferred distractions than sitting with the suffering we feel. However, the gesture that ripens the heart would be to stay present and open wide to this suffering—without recoiling.

Each of us has a heart that cares deeply about the suffering in our families, our communities, the environment, the nation, and in our own hearts. In the Buddhist tradition, the act of caring and tenderly acknowledging ours and others' suffering is known as *Karuna*, a Pali word for *Compassion*. *Compassion* here is not intended to change or sweeten our experiences. Instead, a *Compassion* practice trains us to kindheartedly acknowledge *what is.*

Compassion is rooted in an acknowledgement that the suffering of others is something we can identify with. It is not to say that we feel their exact pain, but rather we understand that pain is suffering and that our deepest desire is that all beings, including ourselves, are free from suffering. *Compassion*—the gesture of caring genuinely about others and yourself—helps us suffer less.

The application is simple. During any of your *Gentling* meditations, when you feel the emotional pain of others or yourself, bring your heart-filled awareness to the experience. Be mindful of not judging yourself. When you are ready, silently and gently repeat these phrases:

- Whatever it is, it's okay.
- Let me be present. Let me feel it.
- It's okay. This is how it is right now.

What gripes our hearts deeply is when we are unable to help our loved ones who are suffering. Compassion helps us to weather these contractions. You may want to visualize a loved one sitting before you, or you may want to visualize your own mental or physical suffering before you. When you are ready, repeat the phrases above and include the following phrase until you feel more lighthearted.

- I care about your suffering.

It's not always a loved one that causes our suffering. Sometimes our hearts are troubled by a bomb-infested village in a remote part of the world, families that have lost loved ones to senseless crimes, the rape of our environment, or leaders of nations who systematically harm the masses. These *Compassion* phrases apply equally to these situations.

Feel free to carry these statements with you throughout your day—not just during your *Stillness Practice*. For example, a dear friend who lost her mother was sharing her experience with me and I found myself gently saying to her: *I care about your suffering. Whatever it is, it's okay. Let me feel it with you. This is how it is right now, and it's okay. It will not always be this way.* If these words do not naturally come out of your mouth, say them mentally. The effects are often peaceful. My beloved teacher, Bhante Henepola Gunaratana, shares that in the days of the Buddha, phrases like these were used to clean the wounds of the sick just before medication was applied. It is befitting that we use these phrases as a salve for our own mental or emotional healing.

Once you become comfortable with the *Gentling* practices, you can personalize them to more genuinely reflect the care you want to impart to others and yourself.

Gentling Practices are beautiful heart songs we can learn to sing to ourselves and others when comfort is needed. We have the inherent power to give and receive kindness. We simply need to practice doing so. So practice as often as you can. Don't limit it to your *Stillness Practice*. Include these gestures in your thoughts throughout the day, especially when your rage child is triggered. With practice, these gestures bring balance, a poised mind, and soft and spacious awareness to our lives.

PART FOUR

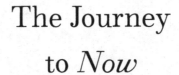

The Journey
to *Now*

15

Rage and Relationships

With a peaceful heart whatever happens can be met with wisdom.

JACK KORNFIELD

The previous chapters were oriented toward becoming familiar with our rage child and the roots of our rage. We will now consider how to maintain healing in our relationships. We will have an advantage if we have established a daily *Stillness Practice* and applied the exercises offered in this book so far.

All of our lives involve friends and loved ones, and our healing affects them immediately and profoundly. As we continue to reclaim our rage, we may discover that we need to negotiate new boundaries in our personal relationships.

Denise, letting go of her *Dominance* disguise, had always complained about being financially responsible for her thirty-five-year-old *Dependence* son, who she felt could never get his life together. The more she complained, the less capable he seemed to become. As Denise moved closer to her own rage, she realized that she was terrified of losing her son and her importance as a mother. She recognized her contribution to the problem, and how she was reacting through her disguise of *Dominance* and its shadow, *Dependence*—complaining, judging, pushing, and paying. With this insight, she set new boundaries with her son, including a phased withdrawal of financial support. During the first few months, her son became depressed. Denise practiced the *Compassion* phrases in her daily *Stillness Practice* as she maintained the financial boundary. Denise noticed that she felt less guilty and less worried, and less provoked into being responsible for his actions. After a few months, her son began to take more responsibility for his life. Denise was finally able to acknowledge and believe that her son was his own person and was responsible for his own life. Maintaining the new boundary had proven beneficial to both of them. Their pain pattern had been transformed.

Changing our own contributions to the problems we struggle with in our closest relationships is difficult, but not impossible. Doing so requires that we care deeply about our own well-being and that of others.

Share your intentions to heal with those closest to you. Let them know how they can support you and themselves. Be aware that others may not understand or want to accept your healing journey. They may resent how you are conducting yourself, and fear that the relationship, as they know it, is lost. Expect resistance, be patient, and stay true to your intentions to heal.

TALKING ABOUT WHAT ENRAGES YOU

The best time to understand rage is not when you are in the heat of a conflict. During these times, the intensity of rage can blind and distort the moment. You may say or do things you don't mean, and feel ashamed and vulnerable—emotions you must quickly cover up with your disguises. Yet, there will be times when you want to talk about something that you find disturbing in another person, and having a framework to organize your thoughts is useful. For example, you may have noticed a pattern forming in your relationship that is causing hurt or frustration, or you may feel yourself growing distant and resentful of the behavior of the other person and want to better understand what is going on.

Maintaining your commitment to healing over your need to be right or to get even is not always easy—just necessary. The following six-step approach is helpful for maintaining balance and integrity when you need to talk about what is enraging you. Consider first trying this approach alone in your *Stillness Practice* as a journal and visualization exercise. When you feel at rest with your responses and can visualize success, you are ready to initiate a discussion about rage. Call and arrange a time. Start with fifteen minutes. When you meet, this is not a time to bring your rage child—she should be otherwise occupied with a nap, not in control of your tongue. If possible sit face to face where you can make gentle eye contact, observe their posture, and hold their hand if appropriate. Use a tone of sincere kindness. Also, you do not need to follow these steps in exact order, but do what you can to include all of them in your conversation.

1. *Affirm what works in the relationship.*

    When we must discuss a difficult concern, the other person is often afraid that the good parts of him or her will go unseen or suddenly have no value, and he or she will be shamed, dismissed, or made to feel insignificant. However, when we start by stating what works and what is truly treasured in the relationship, it helps the ears open and heart soften. There is always something you can genuinely appreciate in another person, and this is a great way to begin. Here are some examples:

    • I value all the fun we've been having together with the kids.
    • Thank you for taking responsibility for our financial needs during this crisis.
    • I treasure our friendship, the ways you affirm me and make me laugh.
    • Our relationship is a high priority in my life.
    • I recognize how you have given more than the rest of us on this project.

- I'm enjoying my work and respect your vision as a leader.
- You are doing a wonderful job of taking care of mom during her illness.
- I respect the choices you have made to improve our lives.
- I'm proud of you for raising your grades in school this semester.

2. *State your concern clearly.*

   Be specific about the behaviors you are concerned about. It is useful to mention things that were observable, and your feelings about them. Avoid interpretations. Keep in mind that your concern is not the sum total of the other person's character or experience. Remember to use "I" statements and avoid statements beginning with *you, why, you always, how could you,* and other accusations. It is best if there is no threat voiced in your concern, like *If this doesn't stop, I'm out of here!* While such statements may be tempting and at times appropriate, this kind of demand will drive a wedge into intimacy. Here are some examples of clearly stated concerns:

   - It bothers me when you shout, then leave the room.
   - I don't like it when you don't respond to my questions.
   - When you spend money that overextends our budget, it puts us in jeopardy.
   - When you threaten me, I want you to know that it frightens me.
   - I know you are angry and I want both of us to feel safe.
   - When you tell me I'm wrong, it doesn't help me understand how you feel.

3. *Own up.*

   The next step is to acknowledge how you may have contributed to the concern you are voicing. There are few situations in relationships where a problem rests solely on one person. Why? Because you are there! When you own up to how you have participated in the problem, it neutralizes what might otherwise feel like an attack. Take your time and give this some thought. It is at the heart of conflict and often your healing. Examples:

- I recognize I did this very thing last month.
- I know I'm not helping when I scream back at you.
- I get scared and feel caged like I felt when I was a child. Then I blame you.
- I know this is an old pattern for me and I'm working on changing it. Please bear with me.
- You were right to point out that I told a lie, and I apologize for becoming defensive about it.
- I have avoided talking about this. It's difficult for me to explain myself.

4. *Invite engagement.*
   Here you open to further understanding of the situation. Don't be surprised to discover some new things about yourself. When you invite engagement, ask your questions—one at a time—then be silent. Avoid interrupting. Calm yourself by silently repeating *Being Now, Kindness,* or *Compassion* phrases. Stay present and listen with your entire body. Examples:

- How do you see this problem?
- How do you see me contributing to this problem?
- Can you tell me what's going on with you when that happens?
- How can we make things good for both of us?
- What do you want?
- What do you believe I can give you that I haven't already?
- What would satisfy you on this issue?

5. *Make a clear request.*

You may have a request of the person, something that would make things work better for you. Requests should be clear, respectful, specific, and actionable, and move the relationship toward intimacy. Seek common ground. Make agreements, not guarantees. Examples:

- I'd like for us to take a couples' class on healing rage.
- I want you to stop cornering me when you get angry, moving close to me as if you are going to strike me.
- I want you to come straight home from school.
- I want you to speak to me only when you feel you have more self-control.
- I want you to knock before you enter my office.

6. *Extend appreciation.*

It takes courage to talk about concerns related to rage, which is why most people avoid them or handle them poorly. Extending appreciation is an important step. If appropriate, sincerely thank the other person for talking to you about your concern. If the discussion did not end peacefully, use the *Kindness* and *Compassion* practices and appreciate yourself for trying. Examples:

- Thank you. I'm glad we could talk!
- This time means a lot to me. Thank you.
- Our relationship is important to me and I want us both to be happy.
- What you think matters to me.
- This was not easy but we did it.
- I knew we could work this out. We are in agreement.
- I'm committed to us working it out—as long as it takes.
- It may not seem like I'm making progress, but it is courageous of me to keep trying.

Use this technique with children, spouses, partners, coworkers, and others, whenever you can see that connection is more preferable to righteousness. If you both feel you are making healthy progress, you can continue the discussion, but make that action clear: *I know I said fifteen minutes and our time is up. Is it okay with you if we continue?* If you feel stuck, arrange more time later in the day or week. However, it is best to schedule a specific time before you depart. Setting the next time affirms the importance of the concern, and minimizes unspoken feelings of shame, resentment, and fear of abandonment.

A SHORTCUT—ASKING FOR WHAT YOU WANT

We don't always have the luxury to plan a tender time to talk about rage. Sometimes we encounter others whom we don't know and/or choose not to be vulnerable with. In such circumstances, we may not have the desire for an intimate or lasting relationship, yet we want to engage honorably and respect the relationship. Still other times, we may have already talked about our feelings with the person and know that they are trying, and even though they provoke us, we trust the goodness of their hearts. In these circumstances, a shortcut is helpful—*Asking For What You Want!* When you ask for what you want, the key is to be direct and explicit. You also want to keep intense emotions out of your request. Don't elaborate, apologize, be coy, or explain yourself unnecessarily. Make it a simple statement, then be quiet and allow a space for your question to be felt, considered, and responded to. Here are some examples:

- I want you to stop shouting.
- I want a raise of x dollars.
- I want to work a twenty-hour workweek.
- I want you to take care of the kids on Monday nights.
- I want to have dinner with you on Wednesday evenings.

- I want you to apologize for XYZ.
- I want us to veto this bill.
- I want your agreement on this proposal.
- I do not want to be disturbed when my door is closed.
- I want out of this relationship.
- I want you to listen to what I am saying without interrupting.
- I want us to go to therapy together.
- I want us to find ways to have more fun together.
- I want a hug!

When you make your request, avoid being seduced into arguing or justifying your request. You might say: *It's a clear statement. Can you support it?* Keep in mind that you won't always get what you ask for, but it is important to know what you want, to ask for it, and to make your request from the heart.

Asking for what you want honors the true character of rage. Regardless of how others respond, stay focused on your desire and take actions that build peace. While it may be uncomfortable to have these discussions, with practice it becomes more natural. Remember: Kindness is our nature.

WHEN OTHERS ARE RAGING

While we have been learning how to comfort our own pain, sometimes this comfort won't come easily or instantly. For example, being face to face with others who are raging can be frightening and can provoke our own rage. While our first impulse may be to dress in the armor of our disguises of rage, we know it is not wise to allow our rage child to be in control. Instead, we may need a "time out" in stillness.

There are other times, however, when we can bear witness to the rage of others without being immediately provoked. We can trust in our knowing—at least in the moment—that we have been invited into a tender zone with a person in pain. Being familiar with this tender zone personally, and having developed some skills in comforting our own rage, we know that a kind heart is required to transform the moment. Despite the disguise of rage we may be witnessing, an enraged individual more deeply longs for acts of kindness, not aggression, disconnection, or withdrawal. It is in these circumstances that we want to practice greeting rage with compassionate awareness and avoiding the temptation to lash out at an abuser who has often been the victim of abuse.

The following information is helpful when others are raging. Remember that you must feel grounded within yourself, and your own rage child has to feel comfortable enough not to react.

Have Boundaries

Only you know when staying present with someone who is raging is a pattern that represents codependence or abuse. In abusive relationships, there tends to be an imbalance in the expression of rage, in which one person rages at the expense of the other, whose self-expression is suppressed, often kept inside. In these scenarios, the person feeling less empowered will often find another target to project rage upon, i.e., her children, coworkers, spouse, partner, even strangers. And often, misguidedly, she expects them to understand and support her outbursts. In healthy relationships, there are fewer rage outbursts because there is more equality and support. If others repeatedly make you a target of their rage, communicate a clear boundary of *No* and stick to it. *No* is an underutilized expression of compassion. Encourage an abuser to seek support elsewhere. If you are the target of consistent rage or abuse, seek help through therapy or a women's organization.

Stay

In healthy relationships, you are in fact building intimacy when you make room for the expression of rage. For many of us, however, when face to face with someone who is raging, our first instinct is to fight, flee, or shrink—to arm up with disguises. I have come to know both in my personal and professional experience that when others are raging, they are intolerably vulnerable from having lost control. Regardless of how it is disguised, rage is a child emotion in desperate search for nurturance. Being left is what our rage child expects and fears most. Yet to have someone *stay* is what the rage child needs. While when enraged we rarely voice this fear clearly, being left can trigger and validate our feelings of victimization while staying could be experienced as compassion in action.

You should *not* stay if you are genuinely frightened or endangered, or if you are in an unbalanced or abusive relationship. If this is not the case, stay. To advance your own journey, the person's rage, and abolish rage legacies, use all of the resources discussed in this book to stay, but only if you can stay in your heart!

Know that your pain and that of the other come from the same well, even though your experiences may appear to be different. By remaining present, it's possible to minimize suffering and discover what you have in common. Here is where your *Kindness* and *Compassion* practices are most helpful. Your compassion and kind attention is often all that is required.

Give Space

The energies of rage take up space, so a raging person should not be crowded into a tight emotional space. As long as you are not in danger, back off and give the one who is raging lots of space. Avoid the temptation to engage. Silently repeat this mantra—*No matter how I might wish things to be otherwise, things are as they are. May I accept this just as it is*—and mentally bow to the pain you are witnessing.

Remember to keep your boundaries. Only you can determine whether your situation is an abusive pattern or an opportunity for growth. Whatever the case, do not permit any physical or verbal attack. Under no circumstances do you deserve to be abused. If the person expressing rage becomes verbally or physically abusive, don't add to it. If possible, take non-harmful measures to protect yourself.

Keep Your Problems Separate

When others are raging, this is not the time for you to bring up all the things that you too are upset about. Don't unload your feelings on their download—let them take up the space. Discuss your issues at a later time—not now. This is also not a time for sarcasm or contempt—verbal or nonverbal—or to try to intellectually understand every word the person is saying. Rage is necessarily messy! Avoid asking clarifying questions like: *How did that happen? Whose fault is that? Why did you do that? You told me . . . I thought . . .*

This is a time to give the other person your undivided, heartfelt, and wise attention. If the person raging is making demands and asking questions of you—inviting you into a tug-of-war, you can respond with brief statements like:

- I want to talk about this, but I'm more interested in hearing what you have to say right now.
- I want to share my thoughts but not when you are upset.
- I want us to talk when we both can listen.
- I hear you. I get it. I didn't realize you felt this way.
- You've got my attention. I want to listen, I want to know.

Put Your Expectations in Check

The raging person is the focus, but she is not the cause of what *you* are experiencing, nor is she responsible for making it better. The raging person should not have such power, so don't give it to her. The reverse is also true: You are not the cause of what the raging person is experiencing or how she is acting, nor should you be responsible for making her feel better. You do not have that power, so don't try to exert it. The point to remember is: Don't expect a raging person to take care of you, especially when inflamed, and don't try to improve or change an inflamed person. Accept them without becoming them and without judging them.

Apologize

Sometimes, we may see that we have done something to hurt the person who is raging. When sincere, an apology can be important medicine to give others as well as yourself. A genuine apology—*I'm sorry! It was my fault! You're right!*—can instantly soften the heart of someone after they are done expressing their rage. You don't want to rush into an apology. When offered too quickly, it can be experienced as insincere—a way to silence the other person, or make things better before rage has had its say. If you cannot genuinely speak an apology to the person raging, or fear that speaking at all is not wise, silently apologize to yourself. For example, you could say to yourself: *I'm sorry for how I have contributed to this problem. I can see how I triggered this. I forgive myself for not being able to do more right now.* This medicine keeps the heart soft and the energetic connection open for intimacy.

We know we are growing wise when, faced with rage, we are focused on our own healing rather than on changing the other person, recognizing not only the other person's rage but also his or her pain. We can learn to look into the hearts of a raging person and empathize with the shame that comes from losing control, and acknowledge that emotionally, we share the same pain.

16

Support on the Journey

As we are liberating ourselves from our disguises of rage and learning how to live in outrageous dignity, it helps to be supported. When we are supported, we can more readily recognize the humanness and universal nature of rage, and balance our perspective. There are as many forms of support as there are people, and the ultimate choice is yours to make. I have listed a few supports particularly helpful in healing rage. Consider incorporating any one or all of them as aids to your healing journey.

SISTER CIRCLES

A great way to be supported on your healing journey is to form a *Sister Circle*. A Sister Circle provides ongoing support for truth-telling and allows the wisdom of your rage child to be witnessed, affirmed, nurtured, and cherished.

If you are already a member of a women's circle, you may want to explore whether an intention to heal rage can be included in the group's activities. Ask if members would be willing to use the methods offered in this book as a guide.

Separate Sister Circles (or Brother Circles for men) are encouraged, as opposed to Sister-*and*-Brother Circles. It has been my experience that the dynamics and effectiveness of groups change dramatically when women and men join together early on the healing rage journey. Often, assumptions are made and fingers are pointed as to who is to blame for rage. Typically in mixed-gender groups, women become too concerned about what men think and become inhibited or angry. And men often expect to be falsely accused and may become indifferent, withdrawn, defensive, or stop listening. This is not to say that similar dynamics are not present when women circle, but women tend to share more common ground in their relationship to rage.

When Sister Circles have met for an extended period of time, it is possible that they are able to incorporate men more successfully, especially if the men have also met in like circles for periods of time. Similarly, women of similar races, ethnicities, sexual orientations, or any groupings in which shared identity helps participants feel safer can circle together and share their common experiences. Regardless of where you land, each woman will bring a unique gift that belongs to all of its members, and everyone will be enriched in turn.

There are rarely any major catastrophes when we join together with clear intention—only lessons. It is my hope that we can move toward circles that include our world family, in which we discover our humanity rather than just our sameness or safeness.

Leadership and hosting should be rotated among members. Starting and ending times should be honored. Meet at least monthly for a minimum of two hours. Weekly or twice monthly is best. The group size can range from as small as two to as many as eight women. You want to keep the size small to build and maintain connections and allow for adequate time for each member to speak. Your commitment should be for at least one year; however, many groups continue because of the deep friendships that result from supporting rage together. Your decision to be in a group means you and the others are willing to accept these responsibilities:

- Meet regularly at an arranged time.
- Listen objectively without judgment or criticism.
- Do not take the rage of others personally, even when it is directed toward you.
- Witness rage without changing or fixing it.
- Do not expect to be attended to when others are actively in rage, thus allowing attention to remain on those who are raging.
- Establish and maintain safe boundaries on commitments, intimacy, and confidentiality.
- Keep time commitments.
- Be intentionally compassionate.
- Be mindful of how disguises manifest themselves.
- Become curious about what you can discover and reclaim in the rage of others.

During your first meeting, openly discuss these guidelines and add or modify them if necessary. The circle's structure should be simple and informal. Rage needs to be witnessed, not fixed. For example, the hostess may begin by inviting each woman to take a minute or two to share how she is feeling, what she has discovered about her rage since the last time you met, and what support she needs from the group. After everyone has shared, apply the tools of this book to address the needs that have been voiced, or tap into the wisdom within the circle and share or create new forms of support.

Be aware that sometimes when people who are healing begin to be vulnerable with one another, distrust or suspicion can arise, along with the impulse to *fight, flee,* or *shrink* to protect us from pain and shame. When this occurs, it is not necessary to depart from the circle or to sever relationships. Often, we are on the edge of a deeper and more genuine connection. Trust is deepened when we risk sharing our concerns without wearing disguises. This requires us to stay with *Being Now*, and cultivate the tools in this book together.

When we can weather the rage storms of distrust, fear, and suspicion, our disguises fade and we form more intimate connections with others. Sister Circles are excellent ways to cultivate a supportive community for our rage child, and to understand ourselves and our impact on others.

Needless to say, consistent and regular attendance is crucial to building trust and group cohesion. Once schedules are arranged, do everything possible to show up. Our rage child expects to be neglected, ill-treated, ignored, and abandoned, and members who attend infrequently may unduly trigger our rage. Make this group a priority for soul searching and you will reap tremendous benefits.

YOGA

Yoga comes from a Sanskrit word that means "union." The goal of yoga is to join our body, mind, and spirit through postures that help tone, strengthen, and align the body. We perform these postures to make the spine supple and to promote blood flow to all the organs, glands, and tissues. This keeps all the bodily systems healthy. A regular yoga practice helps relieve stress, restores balance, rejuvenates the body, clears the mind, opens the heart, and moves us closer to our wise selves.

Yoga is an easily accessible and inexpensive practice that has profound impact on our well-being. You only need comfortable, loose-fitting clothing, a flat floor large enough to stretch out on and raise your arms and legs, and a mat or towel.

There are many types of yoga—Hatha, Ashtanga, Iyengar, Bikram, Vinyasa, Kundalini, Yin, Power, and Restorative, to name a few. Don't let your inability to pronounce these forms of yoga keep you away from this ancient and profound practice. Fundamentally, they all share the goals of health, union, and harmony. It is useful initially to be supported by an experienced teacher or class. Once you have mastered the basic postures with a teacher, you can purchase any number of home-study courses to help you maintain a regular practice. Yoga is a body meditation. It's a graceful way to cultivate inner peace and build strength, concentration, and self-awareness.

THERAPY

On your healing journey, you would be wise to engage the services of a skilled therapist. A therapist can help you examine the origin and dynamics of your rage. Rage can be a messy emotion, and if we are healing, the rage child will not present herself in a clean and polite manner. She wants to be able to rant and rave *and* be welcomed!

I'll never forget the first time I expressed rage in my therapist's office. She was terrified and took what I said personally. Her way of helping me was to quiet me as quickly as possible so that she would feel less uncomfortable. I believe she was also concerned about disturbing her colleagues in the neighboring offices. I felt guilty and confused and angry that I needed to concern myself with her fears *and* my own. We should not have to take care of our therapist or worry about upsetting the folks next door when we are healing rage. It's difficult enough for many of us to express rage, and even harder when we are made to feel guilty about it by our therapists and other teachers.

Within a therapeutic setting, we should have the space and freedom to make an emotional mess and examine its remains. Since rage can be a frightening energy to allow and witness, we must seek safe environments and experienced, knowledgeable professionals to assist in our explorations.

Therapy should not be considered crisis or short-term support but an opportunity for your rage child to unfold gradually and truthfully. Seek a professional who is experienced in working with women and rage and who understands his or her disguises. Choose someone interested in healing the roots of rage, not just supporting you in changing your behavior. Before committing to a therapist, check into his/her background or have a brief telephone conversation. Consider these questions:

- What are your beliefs about rage?
- What work have you personally and professionally done in the area of rage?
- What is your approach to supporting the examination of intense emotions?
- How do you create a safe environment for the expression of rage?
- What has been your experience in working with [Asian, African, White, Hispanic, Bisexual, Transgender, Lesbian, Biracial—fill in the blank] women?

A word of caution: Do not get into a bartering situation with your therapist. For example, do not exchange bodywork for therapy work. This type of arrangement is typically short-lived and often results in an unsatisfying and poorly defined, if not dangerous, relationship. A professional therapist who is experienced in working with rage will not participate in this type of arrangement. He or she will:

- Establish and manage consistent boundaries.
- Balance your need for safety with your need to feel the power of your rage.
- Not protect you from rage but rather encourage you to feel rage in a pure and expressive way.
- Not put you in a position of taking care of his or her needs. The time will be yours!

The result will be that you are the owner and director of this time, with the therapist serving as witness and providing the process and supervision that deepens your awareness and utilization of rage.

Once you have chosen someone to work with, commit to building a relationship over a twelve-month period at least twice a month. Therapy is an excellent way to be supported in deepening your relationship with rage. It is also sacred ground to grieve and to begin to put rage, pain, and shame in perspective with the rest of your life. If you cannot afford the services of a therapist, counselor, or social worker, other lower-cost options include twelve-step programs and reevaluation counseling (also referred to as *co-counseling*). These are widely accessible alternatives to therapy.

INSIGHT MEDITATION

I encourage my clients to attend an Insight [also referred to as Vipassana] meditation retreat. In an Insight retreat, you delve more deeply into the meditation principles introduced in this book. These are silent retreats where you cultivate stillness and a compassionate relationship with your mind and body. You receive instructions on how to be with yourself in kind, forgiving ways, and simply be with things as they are. There are many options for study: two-hour classes, one-day retreats, weekend retreats, or even month-long retreats. These experiences of stillness open us to be more calm in our lives, regardless of what is occurring, and profoundly enhances our healing practice.

Visit the Spirit Rock Meditation Center Web site at www.spiritrock.org to learn about meditation and various study options. For audio and video tapes and books, you may want to visit Dharma Seed at www.dharmaseed.org or Sounds True at www.soundstrue.com. Search the Web or explore what your local community offers.

BODYWORK

Rage is truth born in the body. At the onset of childhood trauma, the complete release of rage was interrupted as we did what we needed to do to protect ourselves. Since then, our bodies have repressed the pain, shame, and fear of rage. As we unmask our disguises, we often reawaken the original pain from the onset of trauma, and this pain wants to be released. For this reason, especially in the early stages of our healing journey, we may feel unexpected physical pain along with the expected emotional pain from digging up old, twisted emotional roots.

When we are uncomfortable or in pain our first impulse is to feel better *immediately*, so we go about the business of soothing ourselves through drugs, food, alcohol, sex, work, or other indulgences and sensations that distract us from feeling. We don't always do this consciously—it's our way of coping. Do what you can to avoid these temptations—they are disguises of rage. The pain you are attempting to silence is not a new problem, but rather an old problem finally releasing itself through your body. It can now complete its cycle because you have committed yourself to healing. Rage naturally releases itself when we open to a physical inquiry, and bodywork supports us on this journey.

The bodywork I would encourage is a touch therapy. Rage naturally wants to liberate itself, and touch puts us in direct contact with rage. With touch, we become aware of what and where we are holding, and how to let go. Touch relieves pain and supports the reunion of body and mind. We can return to a better functioning of our bodies and learn to rest peacefully in our skin.

There is a difference between massage and bodywork. A massage is typically restful and relaxing, and often nonverbal. The goal of a massage is to allow us to feel better through the release of body tension. In massage, we are not necessarily developing a relationship with our body, nor are the benefits intended to last far beyond the course of the treatment, yet it is an excellent way to relax and pamper ourselves. Bodywork, on the other hand, is generally longer term. Through bodywork, the practitioner invites the body to awaken and release, and asks us to examine and understand our experiences.

There are many types of bodywork, including craniosacral therapy,

Reiki, shiatsu, acupuncture, and Rolfing, to name a few. The method I most recommend is the Rosen Method Bodywork. The Rosen Method is a gentle and powerful form of touch. The Rosen practitioner has been trained to notice subtle changes in muscle tension and shifts in breathing. As this process unfolds, you become aware of habitual tension and old patterns are released, freeing you to experience deep muscular and emotional relaxation and greater self-awareness. Says Rosen Method Bodywork founder Marion Rosen: "You become an anthropologist and become your own best discovery!"

Terry, a thirty-five-year-old community organizer wearing the *Distraction* disguise of rage, was in psychotherapy for three years before she acknowledged that her mother's sudden death when she was twelve was not her fault. While she had an intellectual *understanding* of this truth, it was difficult for her body to let go or to feel free of blame. After several sessions with a Rosen bodyworker she was able to *experience* the rage she carried in her body over having been abandoned and was then able to grieve her loss. Through bodywork she was able to move beyond her mental disguises of rage, which had distracted her from transforming this loss. As her body released the pain she had been carrying, she was finally able to grieve and feel relief.

Investigate the various types of bodywork that are available in your area and choose one that best supports your needs. As with most therapeutic processes, committing long-term provides the best results. Ideally, see a bodywork practitioner biweekly, alternating weeks with therapy visits. This combination is a powerful way to enhance self-awareness and well-being.

KEEPING FIT

Caring for your body is an act of self-trust and self-nurturing. You invite your body to work with, not against, you. I know you have probably heard this many times: The body needs to be physical to function well. It is our vehicle—we need to care for its physical structure as well as the fuel we use to run it. This translates into fitness and nutrition.

There is no way around it: Cardiovascular exercises reduce blood pressure and tension, and you need only to exercise twenty minutes three times a week! For example, walking, even at a moderate pace, can transform stiffening blood vessels into pliable ones. Whether you choose walking, running, biking, swimming, or dancing, raising your heart rate for an extended period helps to strengthen your body and its capabilities.

Another component of fitness is nutrition—the fuel we use to run our bodies. You know the saying: *You are what you eat.* It's true! There is a relationship between rage and what you eat and drink. Become aware of how food and other substances alter your mood. Here are a few tips:

- Eat what you love that is also good for you.
- Eat slowly.
- Minimize and decrease white sugar, bleached white flour, dairy, heavy carbohydrates, and caffeine.
- Increase vegetables and fruits.
- Avoid the use of recreational drugs and alcohol.
- Increase your intake of high-quality water.

Our rage child is vulnerable to substances that alter our moods. When we stop over- or under-stimulating our physical body, we become more aware of the moment and increase our ability to rest in our skin.

17

Predictable Joys

Healing rage naturally frees up more inner space for us to feel and be full of life, yet feeling spacious can be frightening. We can be intolerant of our own liberation. To counterbalance these frightening feelings of unknowingness, we can incorporate into our lives experiences that bring instant and predictable joy—encounters that make our entire being soften and at the same time remind us of our connectedness to something larger than our physical selves.

Following are several *Predictable Joys* that I have noticed are especially comforting to our rage child. *Predictable Joys* cost very little, are easily accessed, and place us in the present moment. What brings joy is different for each of us, and it changes. Your task is to partake in as many of these joys as your heart can stand—for the rest of your life—and to be on the lookout for even more of them.

THE JOY OF LAUGHTER

Laughter is the best medicine of all time and provides immediate joy. Research shows that laughter decreases stress hormones, relaxes muscles, enhances our immune system, reduces pain, provides cardiac conditioning, improves our respiratory system, and decreases hypertension. But these reasons are not nearly as pleasurable as the simple and pure joy of laughing.

Make it your priority to find something to laugh about each day. A word of caution—avoid participating in humor at other people's expense. This type of hurtful behavior will erode your own self-esteem and healing. Instead, read cartoons, rent a video, or notice the humor in ordinary life. You may have a friend or relative who is naturally humorous—spend time with that person. Journal humorous stories and insights each day and refer back to them often. Laughter frees up inner space and supports the reunion of body and mind.

THE JOY OF MUSIC

Music travels by air and permeates our senses, creating inner vibrations that regulate our mood. Music affects the release of powerful brain chemicals that have an effect on the rhythm of our breathing, our heartbeat, and our blood pressure. Because music holds such power, we can make use of music as a joy we can count on.

Listening to soothing music can calm even the most troubled minds. It reduces aggression, lifts depression, and improves the quality of rest and sleep. On the other hand, listening to belligerent and violent music may be exciting but may also contribute to hostile, agitated, and harmful states of mind.

Select your favorite sounds and fit them into categories such as: Joy, Bliss, Relaxation, Courage, Beauty, Mastery, Sweetness, Love, etc. When you need to alter your mood, choose from your desired categories. Find a private space to relax and enjoy the sounds. Consider listening as a meditation. Begin with *Breath Meditation*. You might identify a particular instrument or sound and follow its journey throughout the song. You may even imagine yourself being that sound, allowing its vibration to move you or express itself through your voice. Notice what thoughts and feelings arise and ride them. Allow music to take you on a pleasure ride. Kick back and surrender to its predictable joy.

THE JOY OF DANCE

For many of us, it is impossible to feel bad when we are dancing. When we dance, our body and mind work together and we become balanced and harmonious. Dance provides exercise, improves mobility and muscle coordination, and reduces tension. Dance, especially spontaneous and free movements, improves self-awareness and self-confidence, and is an outlet for creative expression and physical and emotional release.

Choose a dance expression that is natural and enjoyable—both are key. If either is lacking, you won't maintain consistency, and in healing rage, consistency is more important than the amount of time you spend.

Linda, a thirty-six-year-old woman putting down her *Defiance* disguise, started a weekly salsa dance class at a local club. She chose this class because salsa was something she enjoyed so much that she would be sure to be consistent. It also offered a wild and joyful freedom that her rage child demanded.

Make a regular playdate with your rage child and dance like nobody's watching. Dance is profoundly pleasurable and predictably joyous.

THE JOY OF HUGS

I get some criticism because I live in California, land of the touchy-feelers. But my motto is: *Hug more and talk less!* For many of us, hugs bring instant and predictable joy! Some of us are afraid of physical contact, but a genuine hug—heart to heart—is a relatively safe form of physical contact, something that can help our bodies to heal. Hugs can break down barriers that words fail to penetrate.

I encourage you to wholeheartedly hug the people you care about when you greet them. Allow your hugs to last a minimum of five seconds! Remember to breathe and enjoy the pure and immediate joy that hugging can provide.

THE JOY OF A CHILD

When those of us who are healing rage make ourselves available to children, we not only witness the subtle unfolding of a child's life, we also awaken to our own. The magical thing about being around a child, especially an infant, is discovering how natural it is to love and be loved. An infant is miraculously one with spirit. Her innocence is pure and her nature unspoiled. When an infant cries, her entire body is involved. Nothing is held back. The same is true when she smiles. Body and mind are one.

You may currently have a child in your life to whom you can open your heart a little wider. Or you may have a niece, nephew, or grandchild you can be close to and nurture. You may also visit an orphanage, homeless shelter, or hospital, or know of a child in your neighborhood. This need not be a time-consuming endeavor but regular enough for you to become acquainted with the child and to enjoy and understand their wondrous ways.

Often our time with a child will help us fill in the blanks of our childhood. We may begin to remember the conditions that gave birth to our rage as well as recall more pleasurable memories. Waking up in this way is a wonderful way to reclaim our own light and innocence. The joy of a child is a gift to all, and an extra benefit to your own rage child, who will delight in interaction with a kindred soul closer to her own age.

Many of us have forgotten that children have wisdom to share. They are not simply here for us to care for. They bring answers to our deepest questions and medicine for our well-being and that of the world. When we invest in the well-being of a child, we discover how to love, how to forgive, and how to live in the moment. Of course it is not always sugar and spice, but it is always real and often joyful.

THE JOY OF A TEENAGER

Teenagers know the truth about their bodies even in the midst of being programmed out of it. They are on fire, candid, often uninhibited, creative, and wise—things we are reclaiming within ourselves. What is often missing from a teenager's life is respectful attention to truth and inner freedom. Teenagers need to be around creative people, and around role models who practice what they preach, and most parents would appreciate this support.

It can be joyous to cultivate a relationship with a teenager and his or her family, and encourage an atmosphere of nonjudgment, creativity, and service. Make an agreement with the family to be of service. Offer assistance with homework, reading, cultural experiences, or exposure to your line of work or special interest. Every teenager should be able to look back on her life and say: *There was this woman who loved me, and I could be myself with her. She saw my potential. She really tried to know me for who I truly was.*

Many teenagers embody those qualities that we have lost and now seek to reclaim—audaciousness, naturalness, timelessness, innocence, and sexual freedom. Enjoy the charge of being around a teen and awaken to who you are. When we take advantage of this predictable joy, we rediscover and advance those parts of ourselves that have always been free.

THE JOY OF AN ELDER

Many of us have difficult relationships with elders in our bloodline. We may have lost them too early, never knew them, or they may still be alive but there may be a painful estrangement due to regret or disappointment. We may even push them to the side or avoid them because we may not be able to tolerate their pain and suffering.

When we feel cut off from our elders, we miss out on the sacred wisdom of their lives and the human experience of aging, death, and dying. Being able to be present with both the joy and complexity of our elders is part of becoming present with our full selves. Just as a child reminds us of our birth, youth, and innocence, many elders embody grace and wisdom that can teach us how to navigate our lives. Unfortunately many elders die alone, with their wisdom unexplored. Being unable or unwilling to draw upon their vast stores of wisdom is a profound disservice to our evolution and dwarfs our experiences of joy.

To experience this joy, identify an elder with whom you want to develop a deeper connection. Perhaps it's your own parents, or an older person in a nursing home or a hospital, a neighbor, or a friend's parent whom you admire. Commit to spending time with them. The *Empathic Interview Questionnaire* may be a helpful tool to apply. Be a good friend and a good listener. Attend to the elder's wisdom fires and heal together. Edith, an inactive writer, writes:

> I just got back from visiting my favorite aunt. It's been over eight years since I've seen her. She's seventy-nine years old and has chronic pulmonary obstructive disease. It was difficult to see her this way and at the same time it felt like a privilege. To my surprise I discovered that my aunt is a talented writer and

poet and has never shared any of her work. She read several of her poems and somehow they were just what I needed to hear. Knowing she is dying made our time precious. I could see how blessed I am to have time, choices, and energy to be creative. Her words were simple: "Don't waste a minute!" I returned home ready to take my writing more seriously. My aunt helped me realize that I have a writing legacy. She was so happy I came. I've been beaming ever since.

While many of us may not have been able to receive such wisdom from our birth parents, there is no reason why we can't obtain elder wisdom from someone else. Keep in mind that there should be mutual respect in your relationship with elders. You do not have to regress or become childlike in the face of elders. Bringing your full woman-self to the relationship is evidence of respect.

Sometimes, our wise elders will come looking for us to impart their wisdom and encourage our healing journey and their own. One such wise elder, age eighty-two, attended a one-day Healing Rage workshop and captivated the hearts of more than sixty women with piercing truth and love:

> I come to you not out of pity, but from pride and pain. I've kept quiet too long about being raped, and seeing my daughters and granddaughters raped by men in our family. I've stood by and said nothing, did nothing, and it happened to practically every girl child. I was so afraid. I just want you to know how sorry I am for being silent. Now that I'm old enough to be your grandmother, I'm sorry that my silence and the silence of people like me have caused you so much harm. And I'm sorry that I've shut down my heart to life for so many years. I've let you down as an elder, as a protector. I came to this workshop because it looked like a good place to heal. I ask for your forgiveness and I want to state in public that I am working on forgiving myself. I think it is important that we tell the truth and free ourselves. I pray that we can all look truth dead in the eye and do what we need to do.

Healing, at its core, is about returning home. There is tremendous healing in returning to our elders and embracing their wisdom, and learning how to live and how to die wisely.

THE JOY OF SACRED INTIMACY

While many of us are sexually active, the true joy of sacred intimacy is rooted in being sensuous and intimate with a lover, and especially ourselves. Our bodies come alive and naturally respond to contact, but many of us are afraid of our bodies. We may have been physically and sexually violated and have become confused about the sacredness of our bodies. Many of us have settled for sex or abstinence when intimacy—touch, presence, respect, and physical and emotional connection—is what we yearn for.

Your task is to embrace your sexual unions as sacred rituals. Make them an intimate endeavor—every time! Lay with your lover heart to heart, and breathe together. Tenderly examine each other's faces with loving eyes. Avoid talking—it's difficult in such moments to talk and feel at the same time. Holding and light caressing is healing, especially if its sole aim is not to become sexual. If you are by yourself, allow the same tenderness toward your own body that you would toward a lover's. Be fully present, soft, and available without fantasy or distraction. Rest and enjoy the oneness that you have created. Don't be quick to fall asleep—take a long time to rest in this pleasure. It is not necessary to be sexual to find joy in sacred intimacy. You need only to partake in this predictable joy as often and as thoughtfully as you can!

THE JOY OF ANIMALS AND PETS

Animals are powerful spirits. Historically, many shamans, deities, and spiritual leaders are portrayed with animals as totems of guidance and protection. In ancient Egypt, the scarab, dog, cat, and asp were a few of many sacred animals that were respected for their wise guidance. In Native American cultures, many animal spirits such as the eagle, snake, buffalo, and wolf are considered medicine for the soul and are depicted in rituals for peace and healing. Many states in the United States, and some countries in other parts of the world, use animal symbols to represent the spirit of the land on their flags. Like children, animals can teach us much about how to live, love, and forgive.

Consider bringing an animal spirit into your life for the pure joy of it. You can have a pet or visit one regularly in the neighborhood. I'm a dog lover. Brandy, my beloved German shepherd for thirteen years, taught me many lessons about unconditional love. She would lie across my feet, panting and smiling as I rubbed her head and chin. Sometimes I would be in awe at the joy in her face as she looked at me. I would talk to her about life and love and would ask her questions like: *How do you love no matter what?* And she would respond by staying beside me and *being* love, teaching me that *being is love!* I witnessed her growth and death and she never stopped loving me. That was many years ago and I still experience much joy at the thought of her.

The spirit of an animal is where the joy lies. Look around and discover the animals in nature that surround you. Relax into the kinship that animals provide. You will find that your animal spirit has something in common with your rage child—it is your presence that matters most. The more capable you are of *being love*, the more capable you are of *being loving*. This is the predictable joy of loving animals and pets—being love and being loving.

THE JOY OF NATURE

The gifts of nature are infinite, varied, surprising, and generous. Many of us live our lives in man-made surroundings, preoccupied with man-made concerns. But our bodies, our senses, and our spirits have a different home, one much older and wilder. Making time for a homecoming with the natural world can fill our nervous systems with relief and joy.

Nature is indiscriminately generous, and she performs miraculously to a revered audience. We need only be present to her predictable joys. Essentially, we want to embrace nature as an extension of ourselves, and invite nature to help us make sense out of our lives. For example, when you question your worth and beauty, it is joyous to admire in intricate detail an unusual flower. See yourself in this flower. Imagine yourself becoming this flower—soft, unique, fragrant, original—the flower of your admiration.

If you feel ungrounded, take some time to be near a mature tree. Notice its full trunk and deep strong roots. Ask the tree any questions that come to mind, for example: *How do you just stand there through all the seasons of life? Teach me how to survive without hiding. Teach me how to stand gracefully.* Imagine yourself being like the tree—old, wise, solid, and grounded, knowing you have a right to exist. Experience the physical power of this natural expression, and listen for an answer to your questions. Imagine *If I were a tree, how would I respond to my question?*

If you feel lifeless and in need of energy to take care of yourself, you may find predictable joy falling asleep in the warm sun and soaking up its rays. If the warm sun is not available, let yourself imagine a radiant sun beaming down on your body, or a beautiful sunset, or a hearth fire. The predictable joy occurs when you allow in more light and become light itself.

If you are hurting because you have a relationship that you cannot mend, invite the earth to join you in transforming your pain. Plant a flower or tree in your yard as a dedication to the person you are unable to relate to. Attend to the flower or tree—love it and talk to it as if it were your loved one.

If you need to grieve but your tears won't flow, take this need to a larger body of water—the ocean, a lake, or a river, and give it over.

Your bathtub will also do. Ask the larger body of water to help you grieve. If you feel overwhelmed, caged, or frustrated, find your way to fresh air and open space.

I take a walk in a park near my home each morning on a long and spiraling path, seldom seeing anyone for miles. One morning, a woman was about a quarter of a mile ahead of me walking alone on the trail. Her pace was fast and she was screaming and cursing at the top of her lungs. I dropped back further on the trail, not wanting to be noticed or to interrupt her self-expression. I mentally bowed to her rage release, knowing she was freeing herself and that the earth and air could hold her.

Begin a practice of noticing the simple pleasures of nature and how they support your existence and reflect your larger essence. Whatever you need, you can find solace and joy in nature.

THE JOY OF ARTISTIC EXPRESSION

When the spider builds its web, it is a mirror image of itself—a beauty we are more likely to pause and admire even if we are afraid of spiders. We can admire the web because of its artistic and unique expression. We are awestruck and wonder: *How is this possible?* We are engaged with the art—the web—not the artist—the spider. Similarly, art provides a natural outlet for our rage child to be seen without being feared.

Our rage child is an artist, and having an artistic outlet is an amazing way to channel passion and express our deepest longings. Too many of us allow ourselves to lie dormant, rather than tapping our creative potential. Art is a resourceful and profoundly meaningful way to transform our rage disguises. Like the spider's web, our artistic talents can reveal and affirm our existence and keep us safe and sane.

Do you long to create a play? Write a poem? Sing jazz? Play the drums? Dance like a wild fire? These art forms, and many others like them, are prayers that allow everything we are on the inside to come out. Consider: *What beauty have I always wanted to manifest?*

Identify a creative project—something your heart would enjoy. Sit in your sacred space and ask your rage child to help you determine the most satisfying paths to creative expression. It can be a project just for you, or one to share with others. Be outrageous and don't worry if it does not make sense. Begin with something simple and silly, not something you need to perfect. For instance, trace the outline of your hand, then decorate it with colors or crafts. Then turn it in any number of directions to see what it reveals. Make up stories about what you see and write them in your rage journal. Just begin and be willing to laugh at yourself. Make room to display your creations just as you would hang the pictures of a preschooler who comes home eager to share his projects.

Teresa had forgotten how much she loved to listen to music. She loved the old Motown sounds and would listen and sing any number of them for hours on end. She always felt lighter and openhearted when she sang. But it wasn't until she began a playful relationship with her rage child that she began to write new lyrics to old Motown tunes, which provided her with much humor, joy, and unique expression. Rochelle, raised as a child in an environment of emotionally distant and austere furnishings, realized through her relationship with her rage child that her attraction to quilting was more than a casual hobby. It was her way to add comfort and texture to her life. This realization made her hobby all the more joyous.

Your disguises of rage may give you clues about your hidden talents. Melanie, healing from the disguise of *Depression*, used her dark times to write poems about depression, giving honor to every detail of her experience. She eventually published a book of poetry that helped others rest and love themselves in dark times. She turned her pain into art and gifted it to the world.

Pay attention to your body's response to rage and explore its meaning through your creative endeavor. Esther, unmasking the disguise of *Defiance*, would impulsively slap her "hardheaded" children when she became angry. During a *Stillness Practice*, Esther recalled that as long as she could remember, she had wanted to grab something hard and change it. Esther found a sculpting class and enrolled. She enjoyed the act of carving and changing the stone, surprised to discover that it was the stone that was teaching her how it needed to be shaped, not the other way around. She was able to translate this experience into the difficulty she was having with her children in that her so-called *hardheaded* children were actually trying to teach her something, and if she looked closely, she might discover a unique treasure not in need of change.

Our rage child is a *fire* spirit—a natural-born artist. Our challenge is to use the fire of rage to illuminate our most heartfelt longings. We naturally feel powerful when our rage becomes tangible and affirmed, even if only for our eyes.

Inescapably, we are both creator and that which is being created. When we partake in an artistic expression, we discover what we need to learn, and learn what we need to discover. Dedicate one evening each month to an artistic project and invite your rage child to participate! The only requirement is that you have fun! You will discover that allowing time for your artistic expression is a soulful and predictable joy!

18

The Journey to *Now*

Rage isn't going away. We will continue to be triggered by conditions that give rise to it. These conditions are both outside and within us. Healing is mostly about compassionate self-awareness—noticing how we contribute to our own suffering and peace. It's not about getting something or changing someone. It's about *you* getting *you*, and *you* changing *you*!

Throughout these pages, you have been encouraged to let go of your disguises of rage, move closer to your own blazing fires, *and* trust that you will be enlightened rather than burned. You have been supported in delving into shameful and disowned aspects of yourself and your family roots, and asked to believe that this painful soul-searching is actually good for you. You have been invited to consider that an intimate relationship with rage can teach you how to love like you have never been loved. You have been told that you are much more than your past experiences, and that the core of who you are has never been touched or damaged by life's circumstances, only strengthened. And you have been given advice on how to utilize your own personal power to rest in and trust the wisdom of your body and be at peace in your own skin. Most importantly, you have stayed with this book long enough to read these pages, and perhaps realize that the journey returns us to *now*.

On this journey, change is often subtle. It may last a few seconds or a lifetime, but the shifts can leave us feeling deeply satisfied. In the early stages, we can expect to continue living a very normal life, but gradually we begin to notice simple yet profound changes in how we relate to rage and those who are raging. We may begin to feel better about ourselves and more attentive. For example, we may be afraid but not feel frozen, or feel the need to blame others for how we feel. As we continue our practice, we do what must be done with less anger, obsession, or compulsion. We can laugh at ourselves and forgive more easily. We can witness our emotions without being controlled by them. And we may begin to notice and anticipate the conditions that give rise to our disguises.

Disguises are like drugs—we go through withdrawal without them. They have served a purpose—they have diverted us from the rage we have felt toward our own helplessness and the shame we have felt from being dishonored and disrespected. As we let go of our disguises of rage, we may feel a new rush of energy. Being less armored can feel as if we are simultaneously experiencing a grave loss *and* a new beginning. Karen, letting go of her disguise of *Devotion*, shares this story:

> I've never felt more alive than I do now. It seems I'm letting go of everything and it's long overdue. My long-dead marriage is now buried. I resigned from the board of the organization I founded. I sold my house and got a smaller one. My youngest daughter graduated and left home. I even lost thirty-five pounds. I feel excited, alone, and at times angry in all this newness, but I don't regret anything that has happened. I sob often, then it occurred to me: All newborn babies cry!

Sadness, even depression, should be expected. It allows us time to grieve and surrender into the deep dampness of shame. Grieving is one way our body rests within our skin. As long as you are not a danger to others or yourself, make space for these feelings. Allow anger, sadness, tears, numbness, agitation, and other emotions to rise and recede without judgment. Avoid the temptation to attach feelings with stories or to overidentify with your experience. Instead, embrace your emotions as if they had no name or history. Allow them to be, without reacting to them. Rest as much as you can and take some time to do absolutely nothing but ponder the intricate patterns of the cracks on the wall. Give yourself a few hours or a few days. Of course, seek support if depression persists. But most often it is likely to be a temporary visitor coming and going throughout your healing.

As we grow wiser in our bodies, we begin to feel more spacious. Our energy is less stuck in self-righteousness or in the shame of our past, and we are more lighthearted and free-flowing in the present. We discover a greater self-trust and spontaneity in our thoughts, feelings, and actions. Our cravings begin to lessen, and our defensiveness and rigidity soften. We are more creative, accepting, and flexible, and we can turn our energy toward improving our lives and those of others.

As we continue to heal rage, our relationships with our children and loved ones will often become more honest. It becomes possible to speak more truthfully without harmful intention, and we like who we are with them. We can claim the power of knowing and giving ourselves what we need.

Susan, fifty years old, disrobing *Dominance* as her disguise and healing from emotional abuse by her father and emotional abandonment by her mother, felt anxious about returning home for the holidays. Her relationship with her parents felt strained, heartless, and detached, and she could not tolerate another year of feeling emotionally distant while being physically close. In our coaching session, Susan created a new ritual. When she telephoned home, her mother answered and she asked that she put her dad on the other telephone. This was her request: *You know that walk we take together every holiday? This time, I'd like for each of you to tell me three things you love about me and I'll do the same for each of you, okay?*

Susan was surprised that they accepted. While she was later thinking of how she would answer this question for each of them, she realized how anxious and vulnerable she felt putting her feelings into words. Asking them the question felt uncomfortable, but responding felt even more terrifying, requiring more from her heart. This anxiety quickly turned to empathy as she realized that if they were experiencing what she was experiencing, it was sure to be a meaningful reunion, and it was. This exercise taught Susan that it was not too late to change her relationship with her parents—she did not have to keep her heart closed, sever her relationship with them, or dread being in their company. She loved them, and she could ask for what she wanted directly by setting an example of the relationship she wanted. At every moment, we have the opportunity to alter our thoughts, speech, and actions.

We won't always be as successful as Susan. Sometimes, it will be necessary to be difficult, independent, insistent, or firm. Our best attempts to be kind or consistent may still result in negative responses. In these inevitable circumstances, we are challenged to return to our *Gentling* practices—accepting the harsh reality of disappointments *and* maintaining an inner and outer practice of kindness. We may begin to trust that everything that happens to us is trying to teach us how to live and learn more honorably.

Over time, we will begin to notice that we fight less with others and ourselves. As we heal, we love ourselves more and need to defend ourselves less. While we may continue to take on certain battles, we are sure to pick our battles more intentionally, staying focused on maintaining equanimity and connection. We recognize more immediately that we don't have to participate in every argument we are invited to join.

The changes we experience may be invisible to the outside world, but they nonetheless have a profound effect on how we feel about ourselves. Life becomes less about what someone else does and more about what we do to affirm ours and others' basic goodness. Joan, letting go of the *Dependence* disguise, shares:

> I was able to be in the hospital, in a really extreme situation, without losing my power. I didn't become enmeshed with my family's negative energy around illness, or devolve into a trauma reaction. Even though the situation was nightmarish, I was an effective advocate for myself, and was able to return again and again to clarity. I can honestly say that there's been a falling away of fear.

People around us may become disoriented, and not know how to relate to us without our disguises. People may bring us their problems to solve, or become angry if they are no longer the center of our attention. Or they may withdraw from us to get our attention. In our rawness, we may at times feel hypersensitive, provoked into assuming our disguise of rage. On the other hand, they may surprise us and take responsibility for themselves instead of projecting onto us. Whatever the responses of others, consider them indications that you are on track with your healing.

Theresa, discarding her *Distraction* disguise, began to change the compulsion to spend, which had resulted in her credit-card debt. Her boyfriend Fred, who was unconscious of his own *Defiance* disguise, became more belligerent, complaining that they no longer had fun together. Theresa was experiencing tremendous confidence in her ability to control her impulses, but Fred was attracted and attached to her impulsivity. Theresa recognized that overspending had been her way of holding on to Fred, and it was not easy letting go of the habit. While she wanted to continue investing in the relationship, she insisted on finding more honest and intimate ways of doing so. They went through several months of adjustment and were able to weather the storm. Their bond eventually became less thrilling and impulsive but more honest and intimate, which led to a deeper and more genuine commitment.

Here's the good news: *It is possible to be fundamentally happy in this life—to live whole and wholesome.* Everything we do to cultivate a loving relationship with rage is an act of courage and cause for celebration. One vision I enjoy is from a story my beloved teacher Jack Kornfield tells about the Babemba tribe of South Africa:

> When a person acts irresponsibly or unjustly, he is placed in the center of the village, alone and unfettered. All work ceases, and every man, woman, and child in the village gathers in a large circle around the accused individual. Then each person in the tribe speaks to the accused, one at a time, each recalling the good things the person in the center of the circle has done in his lifetime. Every incident, every experience that can be recalled with any detail and accuracy, is recounted. All his positive attributes, good deeds, strengths, and kindnesses are recited carefully and at length. This tribal ceremony often lasts for several days. At the end, the tribal circle is broken, a joyous celebration takes place, and the person is symbolically and literally welcomed back into the tribe.

Rage is fuel—transformative energy, the source of our empowerment. Its nature is to liberate us, and its truth mobilizes our deepest, most heartfelt intentions. When we are healing rage, rage can become our ally and teach us how to live *and* love in outrageous dignity. We are free to reveal to ourselves, and to the world, our exquisiteness and infinite potential.

May every one of us become more curious and less frightened of rage. May manifestations of rage be acknowledged as pain and treated with the greatest compassion possible. May we look at one another's rage, recognize ourselves, and fall in love with what we see. May our good deeds open our hearts in ways that heal the roots of suffering throughout the world for all beings. Be well!

ACKNOWLEDGMENTS

Actually, I thought I was done with *Healing Rage* when I self-published in 2004. In my opinion, the book had been wildly successful and I was beginning my next writing project. In May 2006, Laurie Fox read *Healing Rage* while renting my artist studio and felt it belonged in everyone's household—and I agreed. Within months, Laurie, a senior partner with the Linda Chester Literary Agency in New York, had several publishers flirting with an offer. It was right around this time that Alice Walker, the Pulitzer Prize winner for *The Color Purple*, endorsed *Healing Rage*—she thought it was a life-changing "classic." With her blessing, I'm sky-dancing with excitement. Then it got even better. Executive editor Lauren Marino of Gotham Books was eager to add *Healing Rage* to its impressive list of authors and take this self-publication to national exposure. I'm grateful to these powerful women for their auspicious appearance in the life of *Healing Rage*, and for seeing and accepting *Healing Rage* in its purest form—an offering intended to minimize human suffering.

Writing this book was a long, arduous, and amazing journey, and

I received a great deal of support along the way. I would like to thank the creator for the gifts of deep listening and reverence to healing. I am eternally grateful to the roaring whispers of my ancestors whose spirits kept me faithful to this heart work, and to my first love and teacher, my mother, for her songs, soulful wit, determination, and originality.

My work has been deeply influenced and supported by many teachers. Warm regards to Chief Luisah Teish for her ancestral wisdom, and Shaman and Reverend Marguerite E. Bolden for living and teaching through love. Dharma Elder Venerable Bhante Henepola Gunaratana for his fine mind and devotion to service. To my spiritual mother, Dzogchen lineage holder Aba Cecile McHardy, for being the *Friendly Dragon*—seeking me out, biting me with joy, and offering generously teachings of the Vajrayana tradition. I bow in deep gratitude to my spiritual father, Jack Kornfield, for his wise heart, and for being a wisdom weaver of East and West traditions, and for his encouragement and loving attention to my work. Many blessings of thankfulness go to Alice Walker for her integrity, generosity, and wise heart. Also for wise support I am grateful to the Spirit Rock Meditation Center, my Dharma teachers, my family, and especially my *sangha* brother, Jack, and sisters Alice, Arisika, Boli, Marlene, Olivia, Saundra, and Vernice.

I want to acknowledge my clients, who have given me the privilege of their trust, and whose willingness to express rage and understand the unknown in themselves provided me with a wealth of illustrative material for this book. I am thankful to Toni Morrison for *Beloved*, and Alice Walker for *The Third Life of Grange Copeland*—both novels eloquently communicate generational pain and love, and affirm my conception of a rage inheritance. I also want to acknowledge bell hooks for *Killing Rage*, and for her prolific wisdom, and to Harriet Lerner for *The Dance of Anger*, and for being among the first to utilize genealogy in the self-help genre.

This journey has deepened my relationships with friends, family, and life itself, and given birth to a community of genuine support.

Deep bows to Christine Oster, Carol Tisson, Mike Ginn, Alice Walker, Nancy Holms, Hans Henrick, and Suzanne Stevens for offering sacred space for me to write. For continuous support, I'm thankful to Joan Lester, Manly Moulton, Aubrey Pettaway, Eve Robinson, Kathy Ruyts, Monica Wells, and more recently Maeve Richard, Sue Bethanis, Noreen Greenblatt, and especially Penny Terry.

I am further thankful to those who read portions of the original manuscript and provided feedback, especially Jack Kornfield, Alice Walker, Aba Cecelia McHardy, Ondrietta Johnson, Deb McSmith, Claire-Elizabeth DeSophia, Saundra Davis, Erica Kremenak, Ernest Cherriokee, and Cheri Gardner.

A few people deserve special recognition for support during the original publication. I'm grateful to Ayofemi Oseye for providing intelligent and immediate editing, and for being gracious, available, and inspiring. Deep bows to Camara Rajabari for her calm presence and creativity, especially with the original book cover, and to Suzanne Stevens, who has been a beacon of support for many years. Knowing my work intimately, she provided invaluable input that assured the integrity of my writing. While Dr. Delorese Ambrose was the midwife in the first trimester of my writing, Calla Unsworth was the midwife during the final trimester, laboring with me in ritual to shape its structure and ensure translation of thought and spirit. I am grateful for her gentle and generous support, especially in the weary hours. Much appreciation goes to editor Judith Allen, who brought a fine eye for copyediting, inspiration, and faith to the original manuscript, and to Erna Smith, whose joy and generosity reminded me of the importance of my work in the world and in our lives.

I have been blessed by so many that my memory is not nearly as great as the gifts received, yet I am deeply grateful to all of you, named and unnamed, who thought of me kindly throughout this labor of love.

BIBLIOGRAPHY

Bennett-Goleman, Tara. *Emotional Alchemy: How the Mind Can Heal the Heart.* New York, NY: Harmony Books, 2001.

Goldstein, Joseph. *Insight Meditation: The Practice of Freedom.* Boston, MA: Shambhala Publications, Inc., 1993.

Gunaratana, Bhante Henepola. *Eight Mindful Steps to Happiness.* Somerville, MA: Wisdom Publications, 2001.

———. *Mindfulness in Plain English.* Somerville, MA: Wisdom Publications, 2002.

Hay, Louise L. *Heal Your Body: The Mental Causes for Physical Illness and the Metaphysical Way to Overcome Them.* Carlsbad, CA: Hay House, 1994.

Katie, Byron. *Loving What Is.* New York, NY: Harmony Books, 2002.

Kornfield, Jack. *After the Ecstasy, the Laundry: How the Heart Grows Wise on the Spiritual Path.* New York, NY: Bantam Books, 2000.

———. *The Art of Forgiveness, Lovingkindness, and Peace.* New York, NY: Bantam Books, 2002.

———. *A Path with Heart: A Guide through the Perils and Promises of Spiritual Life.* New York, NY: Bantam Doubleday Dell, 1993.

Lerner, Harriet G. *The Dance of Anger: A Woman's Guide to Changing the Patterns of Intimate Relationships.* New York, NY: Harper & Row, 1985.

Levine, Peter A. *Waking the Tiger: Healing Trauma.* Berkeley, CA: North Atlantic Books, 1997.

Levine, Stephen. *A Year to Live: How to Live This Year as If It Were Your Last.* New York, NY: Bell Tower, 1997.

Macy, Joanna. *World as Lover, World as Self.* Berkeley, CA: Parallax Press, 1991.

Miller, Alice. *The Drama of the Gifted Child: The Search for the True Self.* New York, NY: HarperCollins, 1996.

————. *Thou Shalt Not Be Aware: Society's Betrayal of the Child.* New York, NY: Farrar, Straus and Giroux, 1998.

Morrison, Toni. *Beloved.* New York, NY: Alfred A. Knopf, Inc., 1987.

Salzberg, Sharon. *Lovingkindness: The Revolutionary Art of Happiness.* Boston, MA: Shambhala Publications, Inc., 1995.

————. *Faith: Trusting Your Own Deepest Experience.* New York, NY: Riverhead Books, 2003.

Walker, Alice. *The Third Life of Grange Copeland.* Orlando, FL: Harcourt Books, 1970.

————. *We Are the Ones We Have Been Waiting for: Light in a Time of Darkness.* New York, NY: The New Press, 2006.

CONTACT INFORMATION

RUTH KING, M.A., is president of Bridges, Branches & Braids—an organization working with negative energies in positive ways. She offers coaching, workshops, and retreats based on the principles and practices presented in this book, notably Celebration of Rage™. These programs are appropriate for individuals, couples, organizations, health and healing practitioners, and others interested in promoting self-awareness, emotional literacy, and personal development. Ruth King is available for speaking, lecturing, custom retreats, book-club discussions, and life coaching. Visit www.healingrage.com for details, or write to P.O. Box 7813, Berkeley, CA 94707.